the pillow book

maureen burgess

the pillow book

grosset & dunlap, publishers, new york

To Mom, Dad, and Toby

Library of Congress catalog card number: 74-2736
ISBN 0-448-11700-2
First printing

Printed in the United States of America

the basic pillow

the designs

contents

part one

the basic pillow

why pillows ?

1

Every woman wants her home to look comfortable and inviting, and pillows help to create this effect.

A room without pillows is like a sundae without the cherry. It is still good but lacks the finishing touch that makes it really satisfying.

Pillows, however, are expensive to buy in the stores. How often, while shopping, have you picked up an attractive pillow that caught your eye, only to put it down quickly when you saw the price tag? Many times, I'll wager.

But you can make your own eye-catching pillows at home. They are quick to put together, fun to decorate, and inexpensive. You will have something original, made with your own hands, and you will find that creating pillows for your home and friends is a rewarding and relaxing pastime.

A pattern, a pound or two of stuffing, and some fabric are all you need to make a basic pillow. When it comes to decorating it you are limited only by your imagination, so let it run free for a while

create

and see what you come up with. You may be pleasantly surprised.

Pillows also make lovely gifts and bazaar items, and since they are quick to make, you can sew up a number of them in just a short time.

warning   Be forewarned, though, once you start making pillows you will find that you can't stop. You will **see** a pillow in every embroidery transfer, trim, stuffing, yarn, and fabric remnant you come across. You won't know exactly where the pillow will end up but you'll surely find a place for it when the time comes. (If you are anything like me you will have pillows in the most unlikely places.)

In spite of this I am sure you will have many pleasant moments copying the pillows in this book and designing your own.

Although any shape can be used to make a pillow, I have selected the 10 most popular and easiest to construct.

Square	Octagon
Rectangle	Hexagon
Triangle	Quatrefoil
Circle	Cinquefoil
Half circle	Bolster

For most patterns a pencil and ruler will be all you need. Circles, half circles, quartrefoils, and cinquefoils require a compass.

Cut patterns out of brown paper, construction paper, or ordinary newspaper.

Since pillow sizes vary so much, it is impossible to state all possible measurements. Instead I have given the size of an average completed pillow as a guide. Enlarge or decrease the measurements given to make a larger or smaller pillow. Remember, there are no set sizes for pillows. They can be small,

pillow size

medium, large, or oversized, whatever appeals to you.

Inner pad should be 1" larger all around than the desired size of a completed pillow. Half an inch is allowed for seams leaving the inner pad ½" larger than outer case, to insure a well-stuffed pillow.

Pattern for the outer case is cut ½" larger all around. This ½" being for the seams.

Shapes

Square A square has four sides of equal length. Average size of finished pillow: 12" to 15" square.

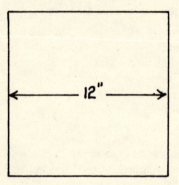

Rectangle Four sides, two long and two short. Average size: 15" x 10".

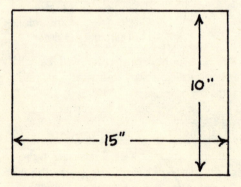

Triangle A triangle has three sides. First, draw a square, measure across top, and mark halfway.

Draw a line from mark to each bottom corner of square. Cut out triangle. Average size: 15″ or 16″ across base.

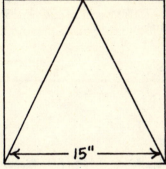

Circle For this you will need a compass. Attach one end of a piece of string or cord to a sharp pencil and tie the other end to a knitting needle or something similar. Cord should measure half of the diameter of your circle between pencil and needle. Hold needle firmly on paper, and keeping cord taut, trace around it with pencil until a circle is formed. Cut out pattern. Average size: 14″ in diameter.

make a compass

Half circle Draw a circle, then fold in half. Average size: 14″–16″ in diameter.

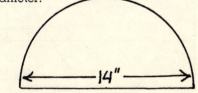

Octagon   An octagon has eight sides. Draw a square and divide each side in thirds. Mark. Join dots across corners, then cut off each corner. What you have left is an octagon. Average size: 15″ through center.

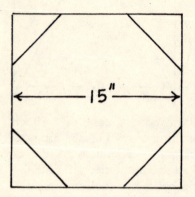

Hexagon   This shape has six sides. Draw a square, divide top and bottom into thirds and mark, divide sides into halves and mark. Join dots across corners, then cut off corners. The result is a hexagon. Average size: 15″ through center.

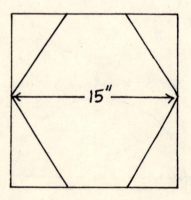

Quatrefoil Four lobes or petals.

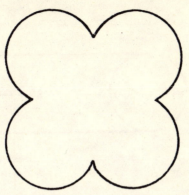

Cinquefoil Five lobes or petals.

I have found that the easiest way to draw these two pretty shapes is to start with four or five small circles, about 7½" in diameter for the quatrefoil and 6½" for the cinquefoil. Arrange the circles side by side overlapping them about ½" and anchoring them with tape. You can use this as your pattern or cut another out of a single piece of paper.

start with circles

Bolster This shape consists of a long tube forming the body, and two end pieces. The end pieces may be circular, square, triangular, rectangular, or any other shape. Average size of end pieces: circle—6"

in diameter; square—6"; triangle—6"; rectangle—
6" x 5". Average length of bolster: 18" to 24". Average width: long enough to fit all around end pieces
plus 1".

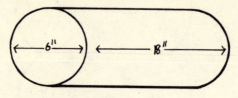

The easiest bolster to make is the sausage-shaped
one. A rectangle is used for the pattern. Average
size: 24" x 18".

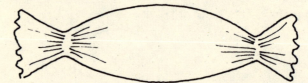

I feel I ought to repeat that the average sizes I
have given are the sizes of **completed** pillows, so
cut your inner and outer patterns accordingly.

3

The array of fabrics available today is positively overwhelming. Shops are literally packed with fabric in a great variety of weights, patterns, textures, and colors.

With such a selection I find it almost impossible to make a choice and have a cupboard full of unused fabrics to prove it.

At one time it was very surprising if you found the exact material you were looking for. Today the reverse is true: it is surprising if you do not find it.

There are the natural fiber fabrics: cotton, wool, linen, and silk. Also dozens of synthetics including nylon, polyester, rayon, and acetate—not to mention the blends of two or more different fibers.

Confusing? Not really, they are quite easy to sort out.

Weight

Fabrics are classed according to weight. They are:

Sheer These are very fine, delicate, mostly transparent fabrics. Chiffon, batiste, dimity, dotted swiss, organdy, and voile are sheer fabrics.

Light Slightly heavier than the sheers. A few examples are cotton broadcloth, calico, challis, chambray, gingham, and seersucker.

Medium Denim, duck, indian head, linen, and sail are medium weight fabrics.

Heavy Heavy fabrics include brocade, burlap, corduroy, felt, tweed, and velvet.

Very Heavy Upholstery material, fake fur, plastics, and leather would come under this heading.

Patterns

There are hundreds of fabric patterns available now and hundreds more in the making. Usually, however, patterns fit into certain categories.

Floral An all-over, even pattern, or an uneven design made up of small flowers, large flowers, bouquets, or clusters of mixed flowers. Occasionally one also sees giant or fantasy flowers. Designs may be natural or stylized.

Stripes or plaids Narrow pinstripes to wide bands, and everything in between. Vertical stripes give the illusion of height and are formal looking. Horizontal stripes add imaginary width and have a calm, restful appearance. Diagonal stripes suggest movement —the eye travels up and out.

Plaid patterns are made up of many different colored stripes of varying widths. These stripes run lengthwise and crosswise on the same fabric.

Checks or dots Checks may range from ⅛" to 1" or larger. Dots can be anywhere from pinhead size to coin size. Dots could be thrown on the fabric haphazardly or lined up in neat rows. Both checks and dots are popular designs, always looking fresh and clean, and never out of style.

Paisley   This familiar comma-shaped design comes from Paisley, Scotland. It is a copy of a pattern on shawls originating in Kashmir, India.

Naturalistic   Designs taken from nature such as birds, butterflies, ferns, leaves, toadstools, and trees. Most of the time these designs are medium to large sized.

Novelty   Fabrics created for specific areas. For example: kitchens—with fruit, vegetable, or wine bottle motifs; and, bathrooms—with sea shells, fish, or bubbles printed on it.

Children's   Designed with the young in mind, although I am sure children appreciate other patterns as well. Ballerinas, cowboys, motor cars, animals, and cartoon characters abound on fabric of this type.

Animal and reptile skin   Animal skins are now being reproduced on fabric. They are really quite lifelike. Zebra, tiger, leopard, snake, and alligator are a few.

Abstract   Have you ever looked at the design on a bolt of fabric and wondered to yourself what on earth it could be? Chances are you were looking at an abstract design. Some of these designs stare right back at you, others seem to rush madly all over the fabric. Usually brightly colored, sometimes splashy, not everyone's favorite but many are quite attractive.

Modern   Big, bold, often splashy prints. No tiny dainty flowers or butterflies here. Stripes, geometrics, occasionally impressionistic designs are found in this group, which is quite close to abstract in feeling.

Geometrical   Large and small geometrical shapes such as squares, circles, rectangles, and triangles cover fabric. Designs are very orderly and precise.

Psychedelic   I haven't seen too many of these designs but those I have seen tend to be multicolored. The colors merge into each other with no distinct dividing line. Swirls, free-form shapes, and splotches roam the surface.

Interwoven   A special loom called a Jacquard loom produces a raised or woven-in pattern on fabric. Damask and brocade are good examples.

Textures

It would be monotonous if everything had the same surface. Texture makes things interesting to touch, see, and taste.

We know what a surface will feel like before we touch it. We only have to look to know that fur will be soft and fluffy, sandpaper rough and coarse, pudding creamy-smooth, and a baby's skin velvety.

food for fingertips   Fabrics vary in texture also. Some, like fur, velvet, and cashmere are soft and inviting. They almost shout out "touch me," and it is hard to resist running your hand over them.

Other fabrics have a coarse, rough feel. Tweed, canvas, and burlap are examples.

Many fabrics are crinkly or puckered, such as seersucker, plissé, and cotton georgette. Broadcloth, organdy, and silk are smooth.

Satin, polished cotton, and chintz are sleek and shiny, while wool, flannelette, and felt are dull.

There are ribbed textures like corduroy, piqué, ottoman, and slubbed or nubbed textures such as linen, bouclé, and shantung.

Some textures appear warm, others cool. Dull surfaces seem warm; they tend to look smaller. Bright, shiny surfaces look cooler; they give the impression of being larger than they really are.

associations   We associate different textures with certain ideas.

When we think of country life we visualize rough brick, earthenware, copper, unpolished wood, and loosely woven fabrics such as burlap, homespun, and hopsacking. These items are typical of the informality of casual living.

The rich elegance of sparkling glass, shining silver, polished wood and fabrics such as brocade, velvet, silk, and satin remind us of the formal life.

Textures are important and one must take care when combining them so that only textures compatible to each other are put together. It is not a good idea to mix formal textures with informal ones (for example, satin and brocade with denim and burlap).

compatibility

When arranging pillows (or anything else), it is better to have a variety of textures rather than many items with the same surface. It is much more attractive and interesting.

Natural Fibers

Fabrics are made of yarns, the yarns are made up of fibers. Fibers are very small, very fine threads from which yarn is spun. The yarn in turn is woven into cloth.

There are natural fibers and synthetics or man-made fibers. The natural fibers are: cotton, linen, wool, and silk.

Fiber	Source
Cotton	Cotton plant
Linen	Flax plant
Wool	Sheep
Silk	Silkworms

Natural fibers only have to be gathered or separated from their source before going through the different stages prior to becoming yarn.

au naturel

Cotton Usually 35"–36" wide, sometimes 44"–45". Cool and absorbent, cotton is a favorite, if not the favorite, of many sewers. It does not slip or fray, it is quite strong and it washes well. Cotton comes with a variety of finishes and is fairly inexpensive. Cotton fabrics include:

Batiste	Dobby	Organdy
Bedford cord	Dotted swiss	Oxford cloth
Broadcloth	Duck	Percale
Brocade	Gabardine	Piqué
Brocatelle	Gingham	Plissé
Calico	Glazed chintz	Pongee
Cambric	Grosgrain	Poplin
Challis	Hopsacking	Rep
Chambray	Huck	Sateen
Chenille	Indianhead	Seersucker
Chintz	Lawn	Shantung
Corduroy	Madras	Terrycloth
Crash	Marquisette	Ticking
Cretonne	Matelasse	Twill
Damask	Moiré	Velveteen
Denim	Monkscloth	Voile
Dimity	Muslin	

Linen   Most linen fabric is 35"–36" wide. It is heavier than many of the cotton group, cool, absorbent, and washes well. It has natural luster and is strong but will fray slightly. Linen tends to wrinkle. Fabrics made with linen include:

Cambric	Crash	Handkerchief linen
Canvas	Damask	Huck

Wool   Wool is 44"–45" wide, and often 58"–60". It is soft, warm, and springy, lovely to work with, does not fray, or slip. Wool felt has no grain—a pattern can be cut in any direction. Some woolen fabrics are:

Bedford cord	Doeskin	Jersey
Bengaline	Felt	Melton
Bouclé	Flannel	Serge
Broadcloth	Gabardine	Tweed
Challis	Homespun	Velour
Crepe	Hopsacking	Whipcord

Silk   Very strong and quite absorbent, silk is also luxurious, elegant, and expensive. Silk fabrics are:

Broadcloth	Crepe de Chine	Pongee
Brocade	Damask	Satin
Brocatelle	Faille	Shantung
Chiffon	Lamé	Surrah
China silk	Marquisette	Taffeta
Crepe	Matelasse	Velvet
	Moiré	

Synthetics

Synthetics or man-made fibers are made from such things as minerals and chemicals.

Rayon and acetate are man-made fibers but are not true synthetics because they are made from cellulose, which comes from woody plant cells.

Rayon   Rayon is strong when dry and is very absorbent. It is also cool. Types of fabric made with rayon fiber are:

Batiste	Flannel	Serge
Broadcloth	Gabardine	Sharkskin
Crepe	Grosgrain	Blends
	Butcher linen	

Acetate   Not very strong or absorbent, acetate washes well and is moth and mildew resistant. It may also be blended with other fibers.

The true synthetics include:

of human origin

Acrylic   Acrylic fabric is relatively strong, not too absorbent, but soft and warm. It resembles wool, is moth and mildew resistant, and can be washed.

Nylon   Nylon is very strong but not absorbent. It will wash well and dry quickly, and is moth resistant.

Polyester   Polyester fabric is strong, but not too absorbent. It is easy to care for, washes well, dries quickly, and is moth and mildew resistant.

All above fibers may be blended with other fibers. There are, of course, more synthetics than I have mentioned here but these are the ones you are most likely to come across.

Fake Fur

I am including fake fur fabric because it is so gorgeous. I am against the killing of animals for their coats but love the feel of fur so I am thrilled with these fakes. They are so real looking, yet they are less expensive than natural furs and much easier to care for. Fake fur is available in black, brown, white, and colors, as well as in animal skin patterns.

Finishes

Fabrics can be treated or finished in a number of different ways. The more common finishes are listed below.

Shrinkage control Fabric is treated to prevent shrinking, or at least to limit it to a certain percentage.

Mercerizing In order to add luster and strength to cotton, the fabric is treated with a chemical.

Glazing This finish produces a glazed or polished surface. The glaze will wear off with repeated washings.

Sizing Temporary stiffening, such as starch, is used to give fabric body. It may be overdone to make an inferior fabric look better.

Moth and mildew resistant A fabric is treated so it will be able to repel moths and mildew.

Wrinkle and crease resistant Wrinkles and creases still form but will smooth out while hanging.

Water and stain resistant A fabric treated with silicones to repel water and stains. Splashes, however, should be mopped up quickly since the fabric is water repellent, not waterproof.

Wash and wear This finish makes fabrics easy to care for, drying smooth, with little or no ironing needed.

Permanent press This is another easy care finish. Fabrics are treated to retain shape and crease without any ironing.

No matter what fabric you decide to purchase, **do** read the label on the end of the bolt before you buy. It gives such information as: width of fabric and fiber content; preshrinkage and colorfastness; washing and ironing instructions; types of finishes; and price. If there is no label, ask the salesclerk for all the pertinent information.

read the label

It is a good idea, when you sew anything, to make a label giving all the above details and attach it to a small swatch of the fabric. Keep all these samples handy in a small bag or box. Tuck one in with gifts you make (leaving out the price of course).

stash a swatch

fillings

4

There is certainly no lack of material when it comes to stuffing a pillow. Department stores usually stock these popular varieties:

Kapok Kapok is a vegetable product. It is inexpensive, soft, fairly light, and does not absorb moisture. It does tend to lump together after a while. It can be pulled apart and fluffed, however, if one has the inclination to do it. (It should be fluffed a little before being used for the first time.)

Foam chips These tiny pieces of foam are sold by the pound. Inexpensive, light, and washable, it makes a good stuffing—if you can get it inside the pillow. Static electricity makes these small chips stick, so that after trying to stuff a small pillow, I look like a snowman with more foam on me than inside the pillow. If you are willing to go through all that, you **will** end up with a nice bouncy pillow.

Foam forms This foam is cut from sheets into shapes. All you have to do is cover them. If you are unable to find the precut shape you need, however, foam sheets are available in various thicknesses so that you can cut out your own shape. Foam forms are ideal for boxed pillows.

Fiberfill If a stuffing could be described as being gorgeous, this one certainly would be. It is light, odorless, moth and mildew proof, nonallergenic, washable, soft and absorbent, and it retains its shape. It is expensive compared to other fillings but it is worth the few extra dollars you may pay for it.

Cotton batting The kind sold for quilting can be used to stuff a pillow. Simply pull apart and fill pillow.

Cotton down This is a delightfully soft filling suitable for small dainty pillows. It can be quite expensive when used to fill a larger pillow.

Cotton covered forms Forms that may be filled with kapok or foam and covered with a cotton case are sometimes available. They are very inexpensive and make ideal inner pads.

Fabric scraps I have stuffed a few pillows with odds and ends of fabric leftover from sewing other items. Pillows stuffed this way will tend to flatten after a while if they are not filled **chock full.**

Old stockings Don't throw away old clean stockings and panty hose—they make good pillow packings. But do be sure to cut off any hard elastic before using.

sewing techniques

5

Before we go ahead, here are a few fabric terms you should know:

Warp, lengthwise grain, straight of the goods All refer to the lengthwise threads running vertically, up and down, on the fabric.

Weft, crosswise grain These terms refer to the threads that run horizontally across fabric from selvage to selvage.

Selvage The lengthwise edge of the fabric usually woven more firmly.

True bias The diagonal of the fabric. Fold corner of fabric down so that the crosswise threads are parallel with the lengthwise threads. Fold line represents true bias.

Prepare the fabric for sewing by straightening the crosswise edges. You can use one of the following methods:

straighten edges

Tearing   Some plain woven fabrics will tear. Snip selvage and tear sharply.

Pulling a thread   Snip selvage and pull a thread, cut along line provided by pulled thread.

Unravelling   Unravel crosswise threads until a single thread will pull completely from selvage to selvage. Trim edge.

Use pattern as guide   A line in a check, plaid, or stripe pattern may be used as a cutting guide.

Pre-shrinking

You should be prepared to preshrink the fabric. Most fabrics you buy today will be preshrunk but there may come a time when you will have to do this yourself. First of all, hand baste the straightened edges of your fabric together.

For cottons, linens, and other washables fold fabric and soak in warm water a short while. Press out water with your hands and unfold fabric. Leave flat to dry. If you hang it up, it may stretch.

For woolens fold or roll fabric in a wet towel or sheet and leave to dry. You may also use a pressing cloth and a steam iron.

Ironing

Before laying on pattern, iron the fabric to rid it of wrinkles and creases. Use a pressing cloth (your husband's handkerchief will do nicely), and have it damp. Adjust heat setting on your iron and test first before ironing actual item. Use the following chart as a guide.

ironing chart

Fabric	Iron Temp.	How to Press
Acetate	Low	On wrong side
Blends	Low	Follow directions on label
Cotton	Fairly hot	On wrong side with damp cloth
Glazed or shiny	Medium	On wrong side
Linen	Hot	On either side
Pile, velvet, corduroy, fur, etc.	Use steam iron over needle board	With needle board or use piece of same fabric as press cloth
Rayon	Low	On wrong side
Silk	Low	On wrong side
Synthetics	Low	Follow directions on label
Wool	Low	On wrong side
Woven, raised, or embroidered	Low— Medium	On padded surface

Machine Stitching

To sew by machine adjust the stitch gauge and use needle and thread size according to weight of fabric.

Fabric	No. of Stitches to the Inch	Needle Size	Thread Size	Type of Thread
Sheer	16–20	Fine #9	70–150	Mercerized
Light	12–16	Fine #11	60–70	Mercerized
Medium	10–14	Med. #14	50–60	Mercerized
Heavy	8–10	#14–18	8–36	Heavy-duty mercerized
Very heavy	6–8	#14–18	8–36	Heavy-duty mercerized
Blends	According to weight	According to weight	According to weight	Nylon-polyester

Choose thread one shade darker than fabric—it will appear lighter after sewing.

Use regular machine stitch for seams and large machine stitch for basting, gathering, and shirring.

Hand Stitching

For hand sewing, use the thread size and type of thread given for machine stitching, then consult the following for needle size.

Fabric	Needle Size	*needle guide*
Sheer	#9, 10	
Light	#8, 9	
Medium	#6, 7, 8	
Heavy	#4, 5	
Very heavy	#1–5	

Here are the five most popular hand stitches:

Slip stitch   Turn in both seam allowances. Pick up small amount of fabric at seam line on one side of closing and pull thread through, then make another stitch the same way on the opposite side, a little farther along. Pull thread gently—sides of closing will come together to form a seam. Stitches should be invisible when completed.

Running stitch   Pick up small amount of fabric, about ⅛", pull thread through, insert needle again ⅛" from last stitch and bring out ⅛" ahead. Repeat to end of work. More than one stitch may be picked up at a time.

Basting   A large running stitch. May be all even stitches or one long and two short. This stitch is used to hold fabric in place before sewing.

Backstitch   Begin as for running stitch but instead of inserting needle ahead for next stitch, insert it behind ⅛" and bring it out one stitch ahead. Repeat

should be long enough to fit all around the pillow form plus 1", and should be 1" wider than the width of the pillow edge. Join ends of strip with right sides facing, allowing ½" for seam. Press seam open. Run a line of machine stitching, ½" from edge, all around both sides of strip. Press under ½" all around.

Pin one side of strip to one side of cover, right sides facing. (Clip strip at intervals down to stitching line, on curves and at corners.) Stitch ½" in from edge, all around. Attach the other side of cover to strip the same way leaving 6" to 7" open along one side.

Clip curves again if necessary. Cut off tips of corners. Turn right side out and insert form. Slip stitch or overcast opening.

Bolster You will need two end pieces of fabric in the shape and size desired (plus 1" all around), and one piece of fabric long enough to fit all around end pieces plus 2" for the body. Fold body piece in half. With right sides together, stitch ½" in from edge leaving center open 6" to 7". Press seam open.

Run a line of machine stitching all around end pieces, press under ½" all around. Clip down to stitching line at corners and on curves. Pin end pieces to body piece with right sides facing, stitch all around, ½" in from edge. Clip curves again if necessary and cut off corners. Turn bolster right side out and stuff. Slip stitch or overcast opening.

Sausage bolster One piece of fabric in size desired is all that you will need for this one. Fold in half, right sides together, and stitch ½" in from edge, leaving center open 6" to 7". Make a series of evenly spaced darts at each end to take up excess fabric. Wide end of dart should be at outer edge with the point toward the center of bolster body. Sew up small opening at ends. Turn right side out and stuff. Slip stitch or overcast opening.

construction of outer cover

7

Cut outer cover pattern ½" larger than size of finished pillow. Allow ½" for seam. If fabric tends to fray, cut pattern 1" larger and allow 1" for seams. If you wish you may overcast single edges of finished seam to lessen fraying.

Fabrics suitable for outer covers will be discussed in the individual chapters in the second part of this book.

Finishings

The final cover can be finished in a number of attractive ways.

Plain Sew as for inner pad leaving a larger opening to insert form.

Buttoned One or more buttons can be sewn on pillows. Not only are they attractive and decorative but they help keep stuffing in place. Cover metal or plastic button forms with matching or contrasting fabric.

With extra strong or waxed thread, sew on buttons by pulling needle through to one side of pillow, leaving a tail of thread on opposite side, slip shank of button over needle. Then push needle back through pillow to other side, attach other button, then tie two ends of thread securely. Snip off excess thread.

Piped   A decorative, seam-strengthening finish. Piping cord is covered with matching or contrasting fabric and then inserted in seam. You can purchase ready-made piping or make your own—it isn't hard to do.

handmade piping   To make your own, purchase enough preshrunk piping cord to go all around pillow plus a few inches extra. If you have to preshrink your own piping cord simply boil it for a few minutes, and leave it to dry. Use heavy cord for heavy fabrics and lighter cord for light and medium fabrics. Cover with bias strips.

To make bias strips, fold corner of fabric so that crosswise threads are parallel with lengthwise threads and cut along fold line. Cut bias strips 1½"–2" wide. Join strips with right sides facing and lengthwise threads parallel, using small stitches. Trim seams to even. Press open. Fold strip over cord with right side of fabric on the outside. Baste close to cord, using cording or zipper foot. Trim seam to ½".

To insert in seam of pillow, pin piping to right side of pillow cover at seam line. (Clip piping at intervals on curves and once at corners.) Overlap ends slightly. Baste close to cord. Pin other side of cover to piped side, right sides facing. Stitch close to cord, leaving an opening to insert pad. Clip seams and turn right side out. Insert pad and slip stitch opening.

exact fit   If you wish, you can have cord fit pillow exactly, without overlapping ends. Measure cord exactly

and add 1" or so for splicing. Untwist ends of cord
a little way and cut out a few strands. Splice ends
together by retwisting. After measuring bias strip to
fit cord, join ends together to form continuous band.
Cover cord as before.

Ruffles Depending on the fullness of ruffle desired,
you will need a length of fabric two or three times
the circumference of pillow plus 1". It should be 1"
wider than the desired width of finished frill. Join
ends of ruffle with right sides facing, allowing ½"
for seams. Press seam open. Fold ruffle in half
lengthwise, wrong sides together, and pin. Run two
rows of large stitches along edge, ½" in (if frill is
extra long, gather by halves or quarters). Pull bob-
bin thread gently and gather to fit pillow cover.
Anchor threads by winding around pins pushed
into fabric.

Pin gathered edge to one side of cover (the right
side), adjusting gathers evenly, then baste. Stitch
other side of cover to ruffled one, right sides together, ½" in from edge. Leave opening. Turn and
insert pad. Slip stitch opening.

Fringed Pin edge of fringe to one side of cover,
right sides facing. Turn under ½" on ends of fringe.
Baste. With right sides facing sew other part of
cover to fringed part, leaving opening. Clip curves
and turn. Insert pad. Slip stitch opening.

Flanged Make inner pad a few inches (2" or 3")
smaller than outer cover. On the outside of finished
outer cover, stitch around three sides 2" or 3" in
from edge. Insert pad, stitch across fourth side on
outside. Slip stitch flange opening.

Boxed Same as for inner pad.

Shirred boxing For this you will need three times
the length of boxing strip plus 1". Join ends as for
regular strip. Run two rows of large stitches along
both sides of strip, ½" from edges. Gather as for
ruffle, on both sides of strip. Use as regular boxing.

Tasseled To make tassels, cut a piece of cardboard the length you want finished tassel to be.
Wind yarn around form according to thickness desired. Slip a piece of yarn under tassel top and tie
securely. Cut through bottom of yarn and remove
from cardboard. Wrap yarn several times around
the top of tassel (about 1″ from top) and secure.
Trim tassel.

Closings

Instead of using the slip stitch to close the outer
cover you might like to try one of these alternatives.

Zipper A zipper is inserted in the boxing strip.
Measure the length and width of bottom of pillow
form and cut a strip 1″ longer and 3″ wider. Cut
strip in half lengthwise, then with right sides facing,
pin and baste 1″ in from edge, along one long side.
Center zipper on seam and mark ends. Zipper
should be 2″ or 3″ shorter than strip. Sew with regular stitching from end of seam to mark. Press seam
open. Center zipper again with teeth on seam line.
Pin, then baste zipper about ⅜″ from teeth along
both sides and across both ends. Stitch with regular
stitching over basting. Remove the basting that
shows and the basting that holds seam together.
Join strip to rest of boxing and use as you would
regular boxing, having zipper at bottom of pillow.

Burr closing Two tapes, one covered with tiny
fibers, the other with little hooks comprise a burr
closing. When pressed together they form a fairly
strong closing. To open simply pry them apart. For
this type of closing allow enough seam to cover
tape. Sew to seam allowance only, before joining
cover pieces, and take tape right to the ends of
cover.

Popper tape Popper tape consists of two tapes,
one with tops, the other with bottoms of press studs

all along them. Sew as for burr tape being careful to align tops of studs with their bottoms.

Sham closing   This closing is placed at center back. Back section of pillow cover is cut in two pieces. Divide size of finished pillow back in half and add 4" to top half and 7" to bottom half (cut fabric accordingly). Press under 1" on bottom of top part and 1" on top of bottom part. Stitch. Press under another 3" on both parts and stitch up along sides. Overlap top piece over bottom piece (right sides outside), for 3". Pin and stitch along sides. Use as you would regular back piece. Pad is inserted through opening and opening remains unstitched.

color and color harmony

Try to think what this world would be like devoid of color. It is hard to visualize, isn't it? We are so used to seeing color around us.

There are thousands of different colors, but they all come from three basic colors. These three are known as **primary** colors:

Red   Blue   Yellow

When one primary color is mixed with an equal amount of another primary color we get a **secondary** color. There are three secondary colors: violet, green, and orange.

One part red plus one part blue equals   Violet
One part blue plus one part yellow equals   Green
One part yellow plus one part red equals   Orange

When one secondary color is mixed with an equal amount of a primary color we have what is known as an **intermediate** or **tertiary** color. There are six intermediate colors.

Red plus violet equals	Red-Violet
Red plus orange equals	Red-Orange
Blue plus violet equals	Blue-Violet
Blue plus green equals	Blue-Green
Yellow plus green equals	Yellow-Green
Yellow plus orange equals	Yellow-Orange

With these colors we can make a color wheel. With red at the top it would look like the wheel shown here.

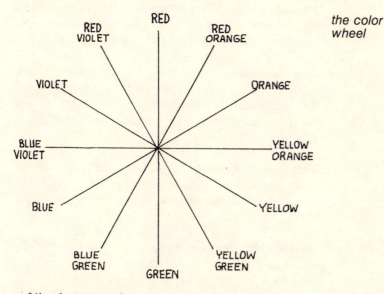

the color wheel

All colors come from the colors on this wheel.

There are many tints, tones, and shades of one color. Tints are colors with white added to them. Pink, mint green, and powder blue are tints. Tones are colors with gray added. One example is bottle green. Shades are colors that have had black mixed with them, navy and dark green are shades of blue and green.

Hue, value, and intensity are terms used in relation to color. Hue refers to the name of a color, such as red, violet, brown, blue-green. A hue can be light or dark; this is known as the value of a color. The lighter the color the higher the value. A color also has intensity, that is, it can be bright or dull. If it is very bright it has high intensity, if dull it is of low intensity.

Color Harmonies

There are certain colors on the wheel that go well together or harmonize with each other. Such groups of colors are known as harmonies or schemes.

Monochromatic   This scheme relies on tints, tones, and shades of one color, and only one color (pale pink, rose pink, red, and maroon).

Complementary   Two hues that are direct opposites on the color wheel are called complementary. The complement of red is green. Yellow and violet are complementary colors and so on around the wheel.

Split complementary   One hue plus the hue to each side of its opposite comprise a split complementary. For example: yellow, red-violet, and blue-violet.

Double split complementary   This scheme consists of one hue from each side of two opposites. Taking blue and orange as the opposites the double split scheme would consist of blue-violet, blue-green, red-orange, and yellow-orange.

Analogous   This scheme is made up of next door neighbors on the wheel—always including **one** primary color. We usually have two choices here. For instance, with yellow, we have yellow-orange, orange, and red-orange on one side; on the other side we have yellow-green, green, and blue-green.

Triad   Three hues at equal distance from each

other compose a triad. For example: red, blue, and yellow; or green, violet, and orange.

Tetrad Four colors at equal distance from each other on the wheel form a tetrad. Red, yellow-orange, green, and blue-violet is an example.

cool or warm

Some colors appear cool, others warm. The colors on the left side of our wheel, violet, blue-violet, blue, blue-green, and green seem cool and have a calming, soothing effect. They also seem to recede away from the eye. Red, red-orange, orange, yellow-orange, and yellow are warm colors and tend to stimulate a person. They seem to advance toward the eye. Red-violet and yellow-green may be either warm or cool colors depending on the colors around them. They contain an equal amount of both warm and cool colors.

texture and color

Keep in mind that texture will alter the appearance of a color. A bright, shiny surface will look quite different from a dull, rough one even though they are of the same hue.

Now, what has all this got to do with making a simple thing like a pillow? Well, pillows have to be put somewhere, on something, and that something, be it chair, sofa, floor, or bed, will have color. The pillow will be part of a whole scheme.

decorating with color

A color scheme usually consists of a main color, a secondary color, and an accent color. The main color is used on the walls, floors, and other large areas. Medium-sized areas such as sofas, chairs, bookcases, make use of the secondary color. Accent colors are usually very bright colors and are limited to small areas—lamps, ornaments, pictures. What better way to add that spot of color, that dash of brightness, than with scatter pillows! They are ideal as accent pieces.

You know, you don't have to be an expert to coordinate colors. Just study the wheel and the different color harmonies, and then use a little imagination. A tint of this, a tone of that, a shade of another can have you looking like you invented color. So get with it and surprise a few friends.

part two

the designs

9

Many of these delightful little pillows were used years ago to scent linens, closets, and lingerie. Others were used to calm nerves, soothe headaches, and induce sleep. Still others were used as repellents against moths and other bugs.

Fragrant petals, leaves, herbs, spices, citrus peel, and essential oils were mixed with a fixative and then left to ripen for a few weeks.

Petals and leaves made up the bulk of the mixture, the herbs, spices, and peel acted as blenders, blending the different odors together. Essential oils were added to enhance the existing scent and a fixative was used to "fix" the scent and make it last. The whole concoction was known as **potpourri**.

Potpourri

It is quite simple to make potpourri at home. Most of the ingredients are found in the herb and spice section of your local supermarket. For others you may have to make a visit to a healthfood or gourmet shop.

ingredients   All ingredients are dried before using. If you have a well-stocked garden (or window ledge), you may want to dry your own material. All you have to do is spread petals and leaves one layer thick, on a wire rack, piece of net, or sheet of paper. Leave in a dark, dry, warm place until thoroughly dry. Stir and turn them occasionally while drying.

Usually about one quart of petals and leaves is needed for a potpourri. If you do not have enough fragrant petals, nonfragrant petals can be used to make up the bulk, but try to have at least one half the bulk in fragrant material.

Fragrant	*Nonfragrant*
Rose	Pansy
Rose–geranium	Bee balm
Lavender	Calendula
Lemon verbena	Violets
Orange blossoms	Larkspur
Pine	Delphinium
Carnation	Cornflowers
Clove pinks	Nasturtium

blenders   The blenders are herbs, spices, and peel. Start out with small amounts of each (one-half to one teaspoon), and increase or decrease according to liking.

Herbs	
Hops	Sage
Rosemary	Marjoram
Spearmint	Sweet cicely
Tansy	Tarragon
Sweet woodruff	Oregano
Bergamot	Pennnyroyal
Lemon thyme	Sweet fern
Lemon balm	Southernwood
Lovage	Valerian
Costmary	Peppermint
Basil	Thyme
Bay leaves	Myrtle

Spices	*Citrus Peel*
Nutmeg	Lemon
Cloves	Orange
Cardamom	Lime
Mace	
Cinnamon	
Ginger	
Coriander	
Allspice	

oils

Essential oils are not absolutely necessary for a sweet smelling potpourri; if you wish to use them, however, a few drops of one or two oils is all that you need.

Essential Oils	
Sandlewood	Eucalyptus
Cedar	Lemon
Orange	Mimosa
Lime	Wisteria
Rose	Lavender
Orange blossom	Rose–geranium
Rosemary	Jasmine

fixing a scent

In order to make the scent last longer you will need to add a fixative. More than one kind can be used in the same potpourri. Mix about one-half ounce of fixative to one quart of petals. The most popular fixatives are:

Orris root
Gum storax
Gum benzoin

recipe for potpourri

To make a potpourri, alternate layers of fragrant and nonfragrant petals till all petals are used. Mix herbs and spices with peel and sprinkle on top of petals. Next add fixative (and oil, if used). Stir lightly, then cover tightly and leave in a dry, dark place for about three to four weeks to ripen (shake, open, and stir every now and then). Assorted jars with tight-fitting lids (from items such as peanut butter, coffee, or pickles) may be used as containers for ripening material. After this time period the potpourri is ready to be put into tiny pillows.

Try filling pillows with just one kind of herb such as:

Hops	Pine
Lemon verbena	Mint
Rose–geranium	Rose petals
Lavender	Orange blossoms

Or you might enjoy one of these combinations:

Rose–geranium Lemon thyme Lemon verbena	Sweet woodruff Lemon–geranium Lemon verbena
Lavender Rose–geranium Rose petals Thyme	Rose–geranium Costmary

Mini Pillows

The tiny pillows are constructed in the same way as regular ones. Patterns are just cut smaller.

Inner cases can be made from fine cotton unless the case is being made for pine needles; it should then be made from something stronger such as broadcloth.

Such fabrics as fine cotton, organdy, lawn, voile, and silk can be used for outer cover.

Tiny buttons, bows, butterflies, flowers, tassels, ribbon, and embroidery may be used for decoration.

color code   Keep colors on the pastel side. Lilac for lavender, pink for rose scents, green for mint, pale yellow for lemony scents, and maybe powder blue for pine or hops.

Any shape can be made into little pillows, which may be left plain or ruffled, fringed, or piped. An ideal size would be 3" x 4", but they may be larger or smaller.

diminuative designs   Here are a few decorating ideas for small pot-pourri pillows.

Butterfly pillow   Decorate a small rectangle of fine

white lawn with three tiny mauve butterflies sewn in a diagonal line across the front.

Daisy triangle   Sew a white daisy in the center of a pale green silk triangle.

Check flanged pillow   Sew purple and white gingham into a small flanged pillow. Attach tiny white flowers (bought by the yard and separated) to pillow, three at each corner on stitching line and one in the middle of the pillow.

Flower pillow   A scrap of floral fabric left over from a larger pillow can be used here. Cut pattern so that a flower (or flowers) comes in the center of pillow.

Blanket stitch pillow   Cut a small rectangle out of gingham and sew as for a regular pillow. Using six strands of embroidery silk in a contrasting color, work a row of blanket stitch all around the edge of the pillow. (See chapter 25 for blanket stitch.)

Overstitched pillow   Make a pink and white gingham pillow. Overstitch around the edge with red embroidery silk (six strands). Sew a red loomed flower in the center of pillow. (See chapter 25 for overstitch, and chapter 29 for flower.)

Ruffled pillow   Make a circular pillow from fine cotton adding a 1" wide ruffle around the edge.

Pillow with bows   Use white cotton with colored dots on it to make your pillow. Decorate with three tiny velvet bows the same color as the dots.

Lace pillow   Use 1" wide ready-made lace trim around the edge of an organdy pillow.

Lace ruffle pillow   Sew ready-made lace ruffle down the center of an organdy circular pillow. Ruffle may be from 1" wide.

Piped pillow Pipe a cotton pillow with white piping and sew a small white, fabric-covered button in the center on each side of pillow.

Half moon pillow Make a plain half moon shaped pillow out of pale colored silk. May be decorated with a small bow.

10

There are certain styles of furniture that are more formal than others, such as:

French Renaissance	Queen Anne
Italian Renaissance	Chippendale
French Empire	Hepplewhite
Adams Brothers	Sheraton

These styles with their classic lines, graceful curves, and ornate carvings call for rich, elegant fabrics—fabrics that go well with shining silver, sparkling glass, and polished wood. Fabrics such as:

Antique satin	Linen	Silk
Brocade	Moiré	Silk faille
Chintz	Printed cotton	Taffeta
Damask	Satin	Velvet

Needlepoint and crewel are also used.

Floral and foliage patterns, narrow stripes, and woven-in designs are mostly used here.

Colors can be rich and deep—crimson, emerald, gold, purple, blue—or softer—pink, gray, blue, mauve, turquoise, ivory, and dusky pink.

The square, rectangle, circle, triangle, and bolster are the best shapes for formal rooms. Pillows can be knife-edged or boxed.

"simple" elegance Although decoration should be kept to a minimum you could use piping, buttons, silk tassels, or silk fringe to finish off pillows. Fabrics like brocade and damask have lovely patterns woven into them and are better left plain. Velvet pillows look nice when they have velvet piping and covered buttons on them.

formal designs Here are illustrated eight design suggestions for formal pillows:

Plain square piped and buttoned.

Plain triangle with six buttons on either side.

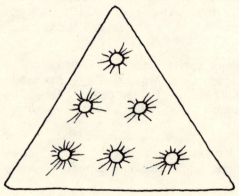

Plain square with one tassel at each corner.

Round boxed pillow with one button in the center.

Plain round pillow with nine button design.

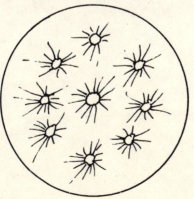

Round bolster with one silk tassel at each end.

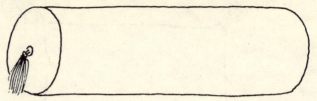

Square bolster with piped edges and button at each end.

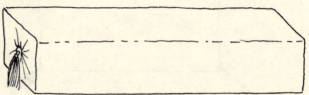

Square pillow with 2½" wide silk fringe.

11

Informal pillows are, of course, the opposite of formal ones. They go well with the casual or country style of furniture such as:

Early American	Rural English
Pennsylvania Dutch	Rustic
Wicker	Provincial

Informal fabrics include:

Barkcloth	Crash	Gingham	Percale
Broadcloth	Cretonne	Homespun	Raw linen
Burlap	Corduroy	Hopsack	Rep
Calico	Denim	Indianhead	Sailcloth
Cambric	Duck	Linen	Tweed
Chino	Felt	Poplin	

Some of the prettiest pillows can be made by mixing and matching solid and printed fabrics. Add a ruffle here, a button here, a bit of fringe or piping and you have some very attractive pillows.

mix and match

Any shape can be used for informal pillows.

Knife-edged ones look more casual than boxed ones, but if you like boxed pillows by all means make them.

informal design tips   Here are a few quick suggestions to making lovely informal pillows:

o Use contrasting piping and buttons.

o Try white piping and buttons on gingham checks.

o Make frill of a different color than pillow.

o Pick up dominant color in a print fabric and use fabric of this color for ruffle, fringe, or boxing strip.

o Cut a single piece of fabric for frill and edge one side with bias binding in a contrasting color. Gather other side and use as regular frill. Binding ½" to ¾" wide should be adequate for most pillows.

o Sew rick-rack trim in various patterns on cover front.

o Have back and front of cover different. One plain, the other patterned.

o Sew two or three small tassels at each corner instead of one.

o Use eyelet trim around edge of pillow.

o Instead of piping use rick-rack.

o Embroider boxing strip or flange.

o Have a different colored flange on each side of a square pillow, or one color on top and bottom and another on sides.

o Purchase ready-made double ruffle and use on front of pillow.

o Use one of the many different braids available for trim.

o Cut ends of bolster from contrasting fabric.

Double Frill Square

materials

2 pieces of fabric 13″ x 13″
1 piece of fabric 4″ x 26″ for frill
1 ½ yds. of bias seam binding in contrasting color
   (½″ wide)
Inner pad

Fold bias binding over long edges of frill piece and stitch with matching thread. Run two rows of basting stitch up center of frill, ¼″ apart. Gather and anchor threads. Stitch frill to center front of cover piece. Complete as for regular pillow.

Such fabrics as fine cotton, gingham, lawn, are best for this pillow.

Tasseled Octagon

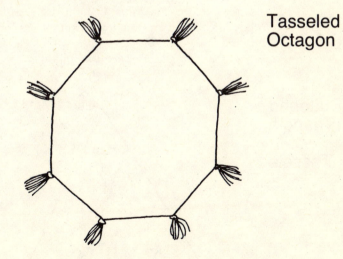

materials   2 pieces of fabric 15″ x 15″
8 tassels
Inner pad

Cut two pieces of octagon-shaped fabric out of squares. Make up as for regular pillow. Sew one tassel to each corner.

Linen, wool, cotton, may be used.

Braid Trim Hexagon

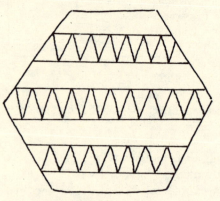

materials   2 pieces of fabric 15″ x 15″
1½ yds. braid
Inner pad

Cut out hexagon shapes from fabric. On front cover piece stitch three lengths of braid—one length across center, the second, 2″ up from bottom, and the third, 2″ down from top. Complete as for regular pillow.

Use heavier fabrics for this pillow.

Buttoned Triangle with Tassels

materials

2 pieces of fabric (triangular shaped) 15" x 15" x 15"
6 - 1" button forms
Scrap of fabric for buttons
6 tassels
Inner pad

Make up a regular triangular pillow. Cover buttons, following directions on package and attach three to each side of pillow as shown in diagram. Sew two tassels to each corner.

Any informal fabric would do here. If fabric is patterned use plain buttons and tassels. If it is plain try a contrasting color for trim.

Cinquefoil

materials

2 pieces of fabric 18" x 18"
2 - 1" button forms
Scrap of fabric for buttons
Inner pad

This is just a plain pillow with a buttoned center. Cut out cinquefoil shape from fabric and construct pillow. Cover buttons, following directions on package, and attach one to each side of pillow.

Printed cottons, gingham, and other light fabrics are suitable for this pillow.

Quatrefoil

materials 2 pieces of fabric 16" x 16"
2 - 1" button forms
Scrap of fabric for buttons
Inner pad

Cut quatrefoil shape out of fabric and construct a regular pillow. Make buttons as above and sew to pillow as above.

The same fabrics used for the cinquefoil can be used for this one.

Sausage Bolster with Frills

 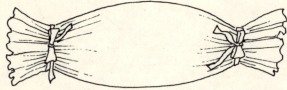

materials 1 piece of fabric 19" x 24"
1¼ yds. bias seam binding
1¼ yds. regular seam binding
2 yds. cord or ribbon to match bias binding
Inner pad
Two small lengths of ¼" wide elastic

Turn under and stitch ¼" of fabric along each long side. Fold bias binding over edge of each short side and stitch using matching thread. Pin regular seam binding along short sides, 4" in from bound edge. Stitch along each edge of binding. Fold fabric, crosswise, with right sides together.

Stitch, 4" above regular binding and 4" below it but not across it. Trim seam. Thread elastic through seam binding to gather ends tightly. Turn cover right side out and insert pad. Slip stitch opening and tie cord or ribbon in a bow around ends.

Use light fabrics.

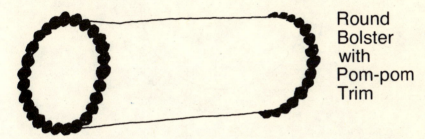

Round Bolster with Pom-pom Trim

materials

1 piece of fabric 19" x 19"
2 pieces of fabric (circles) with 7" diameters
1¼ yds. of pom-pom fringe
Inner pad

Complete as for round bolster inserting fringe around ends before sewing to body.

Any fabric can be used.

Flanged Octagon

materials

2 pieces of fabric 15" x 15"
Inner pad

Cut out octagon shape from fabric. Sew as for flanged pillow.

Use any fabric.

Ruffled Round

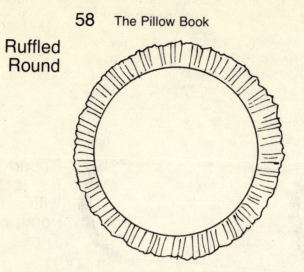

materials   2 pieces of fabric (circular) with 13" diameters
1 piece of fabric for frill 5" x 74"
Inner pad

Construct as for ruffled pillow.

Any light material, plain or patterned may be used.

frankly feminine

In these days, when nearly everything is unisex, it is quite difficult to find dainty, fragile articles that we have come to think of as expressing true femininity. For those many women who delight in the look and feel of laces, frills, ruffles, and bows, here are eight frankly feminine pillows.

Fabrics with feminine appeal are:

Chintz	Lace	Silk
Corduroy	Organdy	Velvet
Dimity	Organza	Velveteen
Dotted swiss	Printed cotton	Voile
Gingham	Shantung	Fur

One of my favorite fabrics is gingham check (especially the rose-pink and aqua colors). A collection of pillows in this fabric is a charming sight.

Small patterns are better than large, splashy ones and delicate, pastel colors are better than bold bright ones. The new ice cream and fondant colors are ideal: parfait pink, violet creme, minty green, peach, or lemon sherbet to name a (yummy) few. And don't forget white.

Although any shape can be used for these pillows, the circle, half moon, quatrefoil, cinquefoil, and bolster are particularly pretty.

Ruffles, bows, buttons, piping, fringing can all be used on feminine pillows, along with appliqué, embroidery, and smocking.

Ruffled Square

materials   2 pieces of fabric 13" x 13"
1 piece of fabric 7" x 98" for frill
Inner pad
Construct as for regular ruffled pillow.
Organdy, organza, dimity, or voile are lovely for this pillow.

Eyelet Trimmed Round

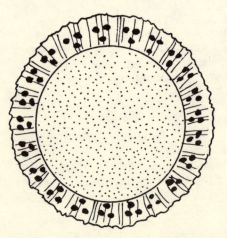

2 pieces of fabric (circular) with 13″ diameters   *materials*
1¼ yds. of eyelet trim (ready made)
Inner pad
    Baste trim to outside of one cover piece before making up.
    Make pillow out of dotted swiss.

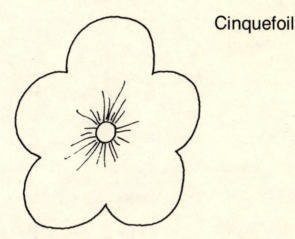

Cinquefoil

2¼ yds. of piping in contrasting color   *materials*
2 - 1″ button forms
Scrap of fabric for buttons
Inner pad
    Cut out cinquefoil shape from fabric. Construct as for piped pillow. Cover buttons as directed on package and attach one to each side of pillow.

Rectangle with Bows

materials   2 pieces of fabric 13" x 9"
Three bows approximately 1½" x 4"
Inner pad

Construct a regular rectangular pillow. Sew bows on front 4" apart and 4" from ends.

Velvet, shantung, silk, or velveteen for the pillow. Velvet or satin bows.

Frilled Bolster

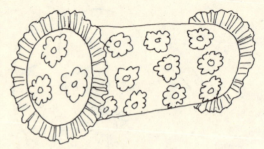

materials   1 piece of fabric 13" x 19"
2 circles of fabric with 7" diameters
2 pieces of fabric frill 4" x 38" each
Inner pad

Fold frill pieces in half, right sides together, and sew along short ends. Then fold in half lengthwise with wrong sides together and run two rows of basting stitch ¼" apart, ½" from free edges. Gather gently and evenly to fit circular end pieces. Baste into place. Now construct as for regular bolster.

Use printed cotton for body and plain cotton in a solid color for frill. Printed cotton may also be used for ends.

Lace Paneled Pillow

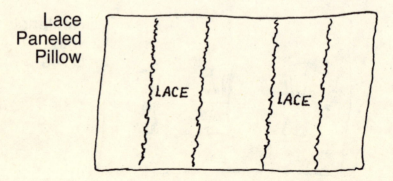

1 piece of fabric 16″ x 13″
3 pieces of fabric each 13″ x 6″
2 pieces of lace fabric each 13″ x 6″
Inner pad

Pin one lace panel between two solid panels and stitch. Attach other lace panel and then last solid panel. Use large piece of fabric for the back cover and construct as for regular pillow.

Solid panels could be made out of velvet, silk, shantung, or velveteen—with the same fabric for back.

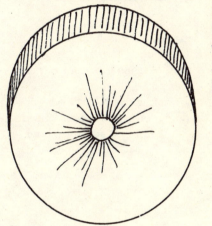

Round Pillow with Shirred Boxing

2 pieces of fabric (circular) with 13″ diameters
1 piece of fabric 5″ x 75″ for boxing
2 - 1″ button forms
Scrap of fabric for buttons
Round pillow form

Fold boxing strip in half with right sides together, and sew along short edges (½″ seam). Run two rows of basting stitches along each long edge, ¼″ apart. Gather both sides of strip evenly to fit circular pieces, then use as regular boxing. Cover buttons as above and attach one to each side of pillow.

Printed cotton may be used for the body, and plain cotton for the boxing and buttons, or fabric of one color could be used for both.

Gingham Square with Buttons

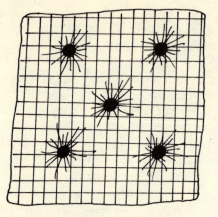

materials   2 pieces of gingham 13" x 13"
1½ yds. of white piping
10 - 1" button forms
Scrap of white fabric for buttons
Inner pad

Construct as for regular piped pillow. Cover buttons according to directions on package. Sew five buttons to each side of pillow.

mainly masculine

13

Masculine tastes are often quite different from feminine ones. Many men do not go for fussy frills, ruffles, or bows but rather prefer strong clean lines.

Heavier, somewhat coarser fabrics are ideal for these pillows.

Burlap	Corduroy	Denim	Felt
Linen	Sailcloth	Tweed	Wool

Checks, plaids, stripes, geometric designs, masculine motifs, and fabrics with interesting or unusual textures can be used.

Use deep, rich colors such as maroon, chocolate, kelly green, teal blue, and gold; or the jewel colors: emerald, amethyst, ruby, sapphire, jade, topaz; and the earth tones: brown, rust, mustard, charcoal, and gray. Strong clear values of red, blue, orange, green, purple are also considered quite masculine.

Use simple patterns with little or no decoration except piping, buttons, or short fringe, and maybe a tassel here and there. Use the square, triangle, rectangle, octagon, hexagon, and bolster shapes.

Fringed Square

materials   2 pieces of fabric 13" x 13"
1½ yds. of fringe
Inner pad

Construct as for regular square pillow. Fringe is sewn on afterward with a slip stitch.

Wool or linen is suitable for this pillow. Try brown and white checked wool with long brown knotted fringe.

Triangular Bolster

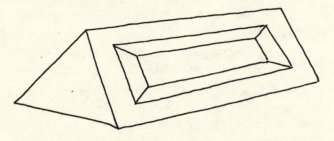

materials   1 piece of fabric 19" x 19"
2 triangular pieces 6" x 6" x 6"
3¼ yds. of braid 1" wide
Inner pad

Make up a regular triangular bolster. Using slip stitch, sew braid onto three sides of bolster, 1" in from edges.

Any fabric can be used. If velvet is used, however, choose a "dressy" braid.

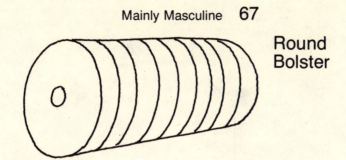

Round Bolster

1 piece of fabric 13″ x 19″
2 circular pieces with 7″ diameters
2 - 1″ button forms
Scrap of fabric for buttons
Inner pad

materials

   Construct a regular bolster, cover buttons, and attach one to each end of bolster.

   Velvet or wide-wale corduroy.

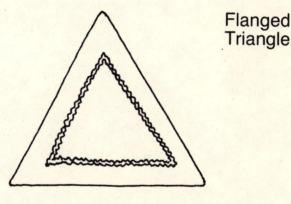

Flanged Triangle

2 pieces of fabric (triangular shaped) 15″ x 15″ x 15″
Inner pad
1¼ yds. of rick-rack trim

materials

   With right sides together stitch around two sides and a few inches in at both ends of third side. Turn right side out and stitch around again 2″ in from edge. Insert pad and stitch across opening, then slip stitch flange opening. Sew rick-rack over stitching on front of pillow.

   Try bright red wool with black rick-rack.

Octagon Pillow

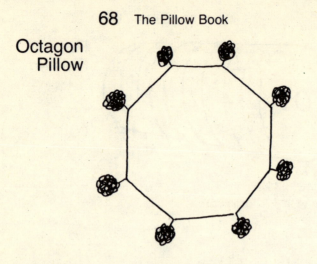

materials   2 pieces of fabric 14″ x 14″
8 pom-poms
Inner pad

Cut out octagon and make an ordinary pillow.
Sew one pom-pom to each corner.

Use wool or linen for this pillow.

Hexagon Pillow

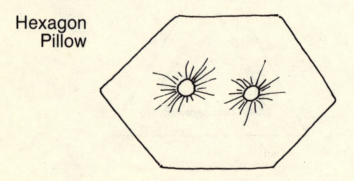

materials   2 pieces of fabric 14″ x 14″
4 - 1″ button forms
Scrap of fabric for buttons
Inner pad

Cut hexagon shape out of fabric and construct as
for regular pillow. Cover buttons following directions on package. Sew two on each side of pillow.

Any fabric can be used for this pillow.

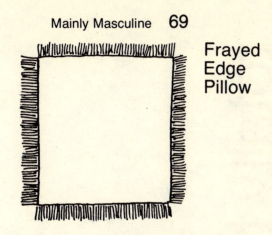

Frayed Edge Pillow

2 pieces of linen 14" x 14"   *materials*
Inner pad
   With wrong sides together, stitch around three
edges 2" in from sides. Insert pad and stitch across
fourth side. Stitch all around pillow again, ⅛" from
previous stitching. Fray edges by pulling threads
out down to stitching line. Trim edge to 1½".

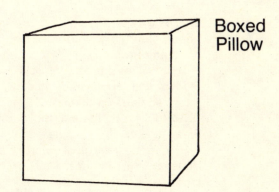

Boxed Pillow

2 pieces of fabric 13" x 13"   *materials*
1 piece for boxing 3" x 50"
3 yds. piping (optional)
Inner pad
   Construct as for piped or plain boxed pillow.
   Use any fabric.

totally teen

The pillows in this chapter are more suited to the young teen, since the older teen comes under the heading of adult.

Teens like simple, unfussy, whimsical pillows. Pillows with road signs, mottos, zodiac signs, or funny sayings on them.

Any fabric on the informal list could be used for these pillows. Fur is quite popular too.

Use bright, gay, alive colors or mixtures of colors. Unusual combinations, such as pink and orange, blue and green, or purple and green are usually appreciated by this age group.

Anything goes when it comes to decorating these pillows. Fringes, frills, flowers, appliqué, embroidery —if you can name it, you can use it. Ready-made frills and fringes can be made into assorted flowers and sewn onto a pillow.

Knitted and crocheted pillows are the **in** thing right now. You'll find some samples of these kinds of pillows in chapters 27 and 28.

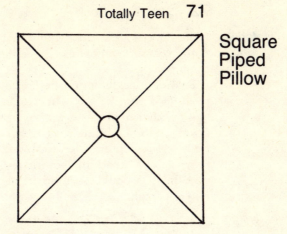

Square Piped Pillow

1 piece of fabric 16" x 16"
1 piece of fabric 15" x 15"
3½ yds. piping
2 - 1" button forms
Scrap of fabric for buttons
Inner pad

materials

Start with the larger piece of fabric. Fold in half to form a triangle, then cut along fold. Fold each triangle in half and cut along fold. Stitch triangles back together to form a square inserting a row of piping in each seam (use ½" seams). Baste a row of piping around outside of cover, on right side, 1" in from edges. Finish as for regular pillow. Cover buttons and attach one to each side of pillow.

If you wish to make each triangle a different color simply cut pattern out of paper first, then fabric. Use contrasting piping.

Flowered Pillow

materials   2 circular pieces of fabric with 13" diameters
Scraps of fabric for petals and center of flower
Inner pad
   Enlarge design to desired size for front cover piece (see chapter 25). Cut design out of felt, cotton, or other nonfraying fabric. Appliqué design to cover using one of the methods described in chapter 23. Make up cover as for regular pillow. Pillow may also be piped, ruffled, fringed, or boxed. Covered buttons could be used in place of fabric for flower center.

flower design

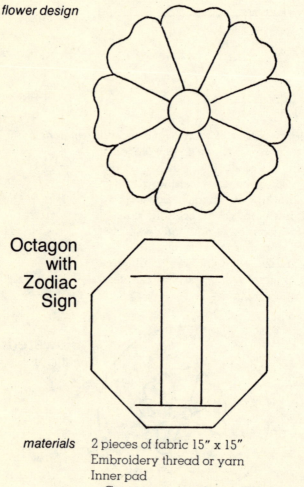

Octagon with Zodiac Sign

materials   2 pieces of fabric 15" x 15"
Embroidery thread or yarn
Inner pad
   Cut out octagon shape. Enlarge design as desired

and transfer to front cover section (see chapter 25). Embroider design in stem stitch, running stitch, or whipped running stitch (see chapter 25). Make up cover as for regular pillow.

Felt, cotton, wool, denim, or linen could be used for this pillow. Pillow may be piped or fringed.

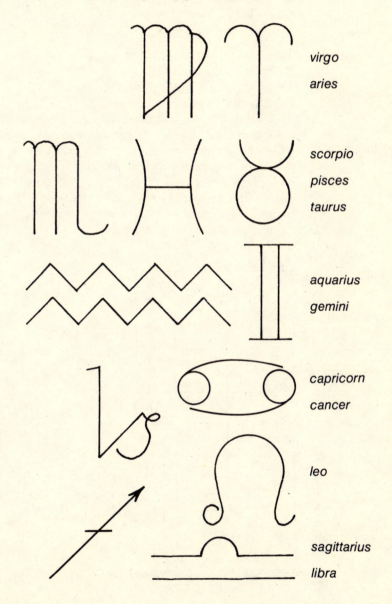

virgo

aries

scorpio

pisces

taurus

aquarius

gemini

capricorn

cancer

leo

sagittarius

libra

Zippered Pillow

materials 1 piece of fabric 15" x 13"
1 piece of fabric 13" x 13"
12" long "mod" zipper with ring at top
Inner pad

Fold large piece of fabric in half crosswise and cut along fold. Center zipper, face down, along edge of right side of fabric (1" in). Stitch close to teeth with zipper foot (Fig. 1). Unfold zipper (face up) and place other half of fabric over it right side down. Stitch close to teeth (Fig. 2). Press fabric away from zipper, then finish as for regular pillow omiting opening. Unzip to insert pad.

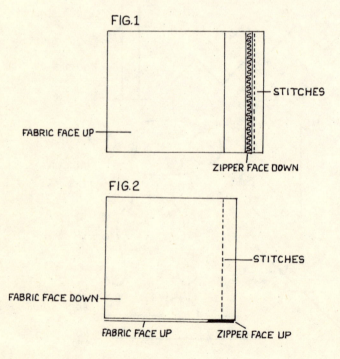

FIG.1

STITCHES

FABRIC FACE UP

ZIPPER FACE DOWN

FIG.2

STITCHES

FABRIC FACE DOWN

FABRIC FACE UP   ZIPPER FACE UP

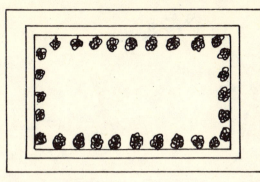

Pom-pom Pillow

2 pieces of fabric 13" x 15"
1½ yds. of pom-pom fringe
Inner pad

materials

   Stitch pom-pom fringe all around right side of front cover piece, 3" from edge. Complete as for regular rectangular pillow.

Rick-rack Pillow

2 pieces of fabric 13" x 13"
1 piece of fabric 98" x 4" for ruffle
1 yd. of rick-rack
Inner pad

materials

   Stitch a line of rick-rack from corner to corner on front of cover. Fold ruffle piece in half, right sides together, and stitch across short ends. Fold in half with wrong sides together and stitch two rows of basting around long edge, ¼" apart. Gather to fit cover piece and finish as regular ruffled pillow.

Bow Trimmed Round

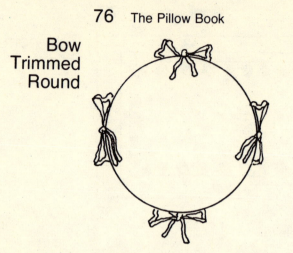

materials　2 pieces of fabric (round) with 13" diameters
4 - 20" long pieces of thick yarn
Inner pad

Make up a regular circular pillow. Sew middle 9" of each piece of yarn to edge of pillow with slip stitches. Tie ends in bows. Snip off any excess yarn.

Patchwork Pillow

materials　32 - 4" x 4" squares, all different
1 piece of fabric for frill 98" x 7" (plain)
Inner pad

Sew 16 patches together using ½" seams for front cover. Repeat this for back cover. Fold frill piece in half with right sides together and stitch across short ends. Fold in half with wrong sides together and baste around long edge, two rows of basting ¼" apart. Finish as for regular ruffled pillow.

children's charmers

15

Some children couldn't care less what kind of things go into their rooms; others have very definite ideas and voice them readily and in no uncertain terms.

A child's room is usually a play room, so pillows should be able to take a good deal of wear and tear. They should be strong enough to be handled roughly, sat on, eaten on, stood on, knelt on, even written on, and definitely thrown (there is nothing like a good pillow fight).

There is no place in a child's room for **no touch** pillows. Children love to touch things, and should be allowed to feel and enjoy a variety of textures—the crispness of cotton, the softness of fur, the smoothness of velvet, and the roughness of burlap and canvas. You can make a lot of pillows, in a variety of inexpensive fabrics, with different textures, for a small amount of money. (I couldn't believe it when I saw children's pillows in a big department store, selling for $10.98 each!)

Sturdy, washable fabrics are best for children's pillows.

Burlap   Corduroy   Cottons
Denim   Duck   Felt
Linen   Sailcloth

Patterns can be quite varied, not just childish prints.

Checks   Floral
Polka dots Naturalistic
Stripes   Geometric
Plaids   Psychedelic

Children love color—bright color and lots of it. Fire-engine red, electric blue, sunny yellow, bright orange are happy, lively colors, and children are at home with them. Most turn away from dull, drab colors, and dark colors are only popular with mothers whose main concern is that they don't get dirty as fast.

For the young set, plain pillows or pillows decorated with embroidery, appliqué, or piping are best. In short, use decorations that can't be accidently (or otherwise) ripped off, and, in the case of very young children, swallowed.

All shapes may be used for these pillows and giant pillows are great for kiddies too.

Keep in mind that there are nonallergenic stuffings on the market should you have a child or friend who is allergic to certain things. Read the label to be sure the one you are buying **is** nonallergenic. You will have to pay extra for such stuffing but it is worth it.

Here are eight children's charmers for you to copy.

Alphabet Bolster

materials 1 piece of fabric 21" x 13"
2 square pieces of fabric 6" x 6"
Embroidery thread
Inner pad

Embroider 24 letters of the alphabet on front of large piece of fabric, and one letter on each end piece. Use stem stitch. Make up pillow as for regular bolster. When working letters of the alphabet, leave 1" free of embroidery all around piece of fabric.

Funny Face Pillow

materials 2 pieces of felt (triangular shaped) 15" x 16" x 16"
Scraps of felt for face
Approximately 1 oz. of double knit yarn cut into
     6" lengths
Inner pad

Cut off top of triangle 2" from point.

Cut facial features out of scraps of felt and appliqué to one side of cover piece. See chapter 23 for appliqué method.

Stitch half of yarn to inside of top of triangle as shown.

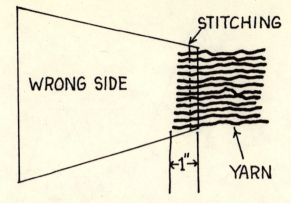

Repeat on other piece.

With wrong sides together, sew cover along the two sides, turn right side out, insert pad, and slip stitch bottom.

funny face pattern

Sad and Happy Pillow

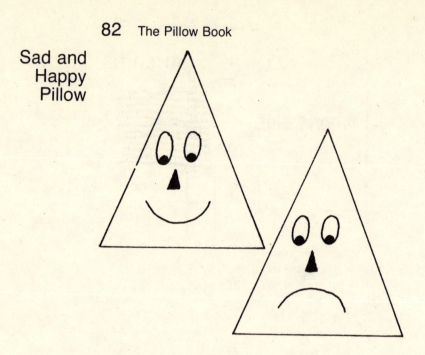

materials 2 pieces of fabric (triangular shaped) 15" x 15" x 15"
Embroidery thread for face and around pillow
Inner pad

Embroider sad face on one cover piece and a happy face on the other piece. For sad face use **funny face** pattern omitting teeth and eyes and turning mouth up-side-down. Use eye pattern below. For happy face use nose and mouth pattern for **funny face,** omit teeth, and use eye pattern below. With wrong sides together work buttonhole stitch around edge of pillow cover leaving opening. Insert pad and work buttonhole stitch over opening.

*eyes
pattern*

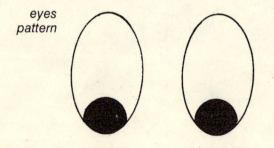

Baseball Mitt Pillow

materials

2 pieces of fabric 14″ x 14″
Embroidery thread
Stuffing

Enlarge pattern and cut out of fabric. Embroider half moon in stem stitch or running stitch. With wrong sides together sew around mitt leaving bottom open for stuffing. Stuff and slip stitch opening.

mitt

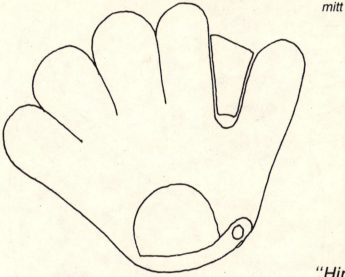

"Hippy Potamus" Pillow

materials

2 pieces of fabric 13″ x 15″
1 piece of fabric 11″ x 13″ for hippo
Embroidery thread
Stuffing

Cut out hippo (enlarge if you wish to). Appliqué onto front cover piece. Embroider eyes, nose, mouth, and ears in stem stitch. Work center of eye in satin stitch. Flowers are worked in straight stitch. Grass is embroidered in stem stitch. Make up as for regular pillow and stuff.

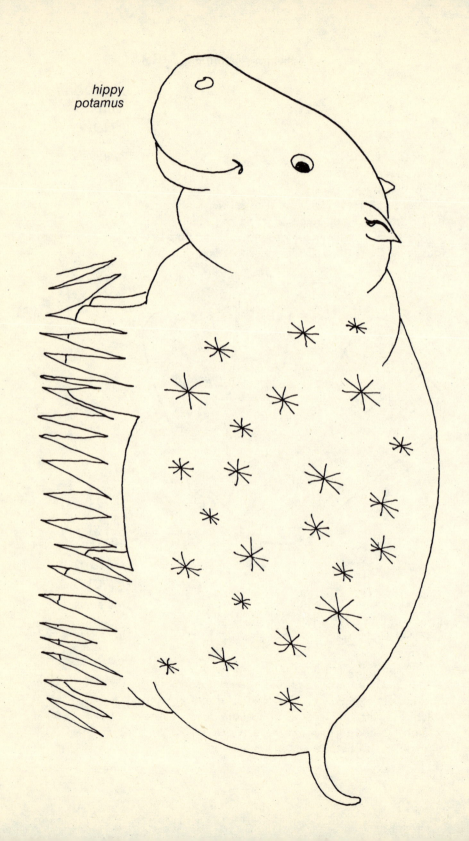

hippy
potamus

Caterpillar Pillow

materials

2 pieces of fabric each 18" x 11"
Scraps of fabric for caterpillar
Embroidery thread
Inner pad

Cut out eight circles from scraps of fabric, each with 2½" diameters. Arrange on front pillow piece as shown below. Overstitch in place.

Embroider face on first circle and two pairs of legs on others. Mouth, feelers, and legs are worked in stem stitch. Nose, eyes, and tail are done in satin stitch. Tail goes on last circle. With right sides together, sew around three sides of cover. Turn right side out and insert pad, sew up opening.

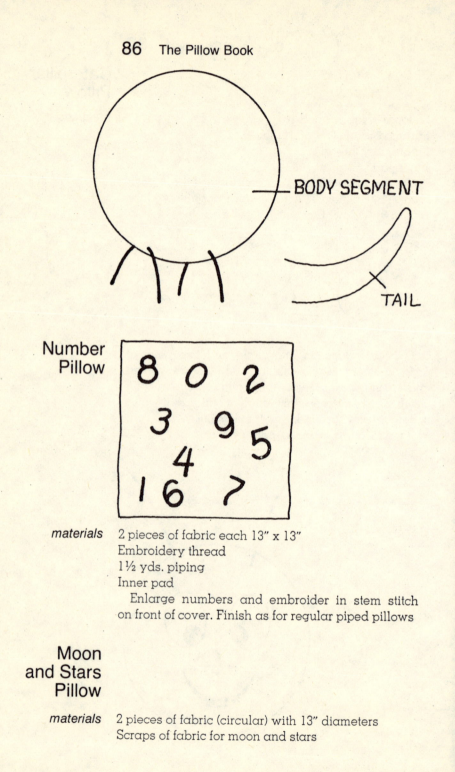

BODY SEGMENT

TAIL

Number Pillow

materials   2 pieces of fabric each 13" x 13"
Embroidery thread
1½ yds. piping
Inner pad
   Enlarge numbers and embroider in stem stitch on front of cover. Finish as for regular piped pillows

Moon and Stars Pillow

materials   2 pieces of fabric (circular) with 13" diameters
Scraps of fabric for moon and stars

Embroidery thread for moon's face
1¼ yds. piping
Inner pad
   Appliqué moon to the center of front cover piece.
Embroider face on moon in stem or running stitch.
Appliqué stars around moon, use as many as you
like. Make up as for regular piped pillow.

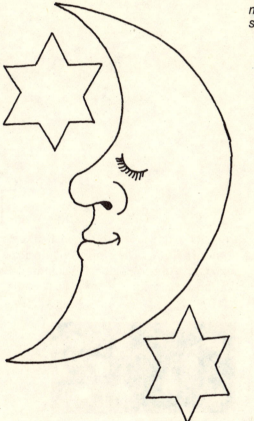

*moon and
stars pattern*

novelty pillows

16

Novelty pillows are really just an extension of informal pillows. They are fun to make for gifts or bazaars. Any fabric on the informal list would do for these pillows.

Domino Pillow

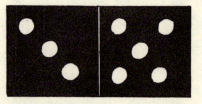

materials
2 pieces of fabric each 15" x 9"
White felt for spots
Piece of fabric 50" x 2" for boxing
Inner pad
    Cut out eight, 1" diameter circles. Arrange on front cover piece as shown in drawing and sew on with overstitching. Make up as for regular boxed pillow.

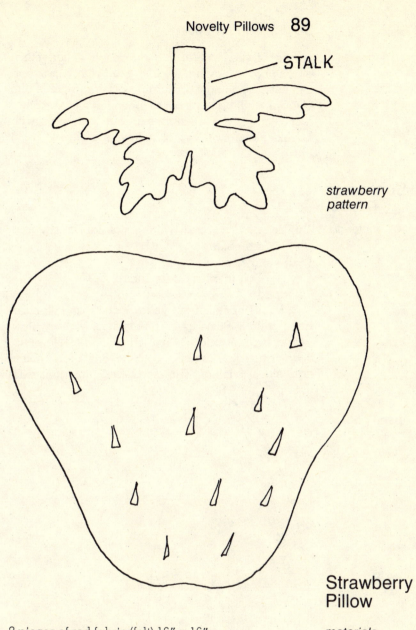

STALK

strawberry pattern

Strawberry Pillow

materials

2 pieces of red fabric (felt) 16" x 16"
1 small piece of green felt
Embroidery thread, black
Kapok

  Enlarge design and cut from red felt. Embroider
"specks" on strawberry in satin stitch on both

pieces of fabric. With right sides together, stitch around cover leaving opening. Stuff with kapok and slip stitch opening after turning cover right side out. Cut two stalk patterns out of green felt. Sew together along top only. Turn right side out, stuff stalk with kapok. Place over top of pillow and slip stitch in place.

Sunflower Pillow

materials 2 pieces of black and white check fabric (circular) with 11" diameters
1 yd. yellow cotton
½ yd. pellon interfacing (optional)
Inner pad

Cut out 16 petals from yellow cotton, and 8 petals from pellon. Baste pellon petals to eight yellow petals (wrong side). Make darts in all 16 petals. Sew one pellon-covered petal to one plain petal, right sides together. Trim seam and turn right side out.

petal pattern

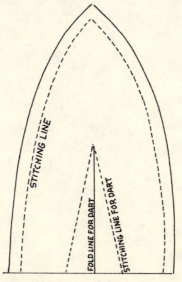

Press. Arrange petals, sides overlapping slightly, on right side of one circle. Bottom edge of petals should be at outer edge of circle. Baste in place one inch from edge. Finish as for regular pillow.

materials

2 pieces of fabric 15" x 11"
Scraps of fabric
Embroidery thread
Inner pad

Cut out six large diamonds (or other motif) and four small ones. Embroider the number 3 in two opposite corners on both cover pieces. Sew one small diamond under each number. Sew three large diamonds 1" apart and 1" from top and bottom, down center of both cover pieces. Finish as for regular pillow.

card motifs

club motif

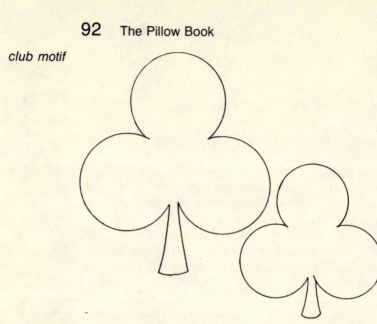

Leaf
Pillow

materials   2 pieces of fabric 18" x 15"
Embroidery thread, brown
Inner pad or stuffing

   Enlarge leaf pattern and cut out of fabric. Embroider veins in stem stitch. With right sides together sew around cover leaving opening. Insert pad or stuff, sew up opening. Use ½" seams.

leaf pattern

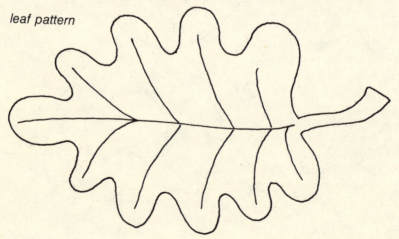

17

As mentioned earlier there are many fun furs on the market. Fake yet so real looking, you can make your choice from:

Zebra	Tiger	Seal
Beaver	Ocelot	Leopard
Mink	Lamb	Sheep

There are also plain fur fabrics in black, white, and colors.

Some of these fabrics can be washed at home, others have to be dry cleaned. Read the label carefully before you buy, then you will have no problems when it comes to cleaning time.

For fur pillows, plain shapes such as the square, rectangle, triangle, and circle are best. The pillows may be boxed or knife edged. No decoration is needed because the fabric is attractive enough left plain. Giant fur pillows are a luxury—but what a luxury!

Remember that people love to touch fur, so be

prepared to have your pillows handled. By the way, if you have someone in your home who loves to read the paper while relaxing on the cushions, don't make your pillows out of white fur. The ink from the newspaper will rub off onto the fur and in a surprisingly short time you will have gray pillows, and not a nice gray.

I have not given instructions for individual pillows because fur pillows are much better left plain and the directions for plain pillows are given earlier in the book. Simply decide what size pillow you want to make and cut out your pattern. There are, however, a few tricks to remember when you are working with fur fabric:

1. For cutting, place your pattern against the back of the fabric.
2. Use a razor blade or the point of a sharp pair of scissors and slice through the back of the fabric only. (You will not cut the fur fibers this way.)
3. After sewing, pry out any fibers that get caught in the seam with a toothpick or pinhead, then gently brush and fluff fur to hide seam and **groom** pillow.

beach pillows

Pillows for the beach and pool area should be made from completely washable fabrics and fillings, for obvious reasons. They will probably end up with a dunking sometime or another.

Terrycloth, denim, duck, sailcloth, cotton, and gingham are good choices for beach pillows. Foam makes a good filling and a kapok-filled pillow will float for a while if it is dropped in the pool.

Colors should be bright, vivid, happy, and alive. The best patterns include large flowers, sea shells, fish, dots, stripes, checks, and nautical designs.

Plain or piped pillows are best suited for the beach, as it is hard to shake sand out of frills and fringes. However, if you use gaily-colored fabric or cheerful patterns you can still make very attractive pillows. Hand towels sometimes have unusual designs on them and two towels can make a lovely big pillow. Of course, pillows may be embroidered, or appliquéd, and patchwork is nice too.

Triangle Pillow

materials   2 pieces of triangular-shaped fabric 15" x 15" x 15"
1 piece of fabric 2" x 10"
Inner pad

Snip top off triangle 1" from point. Fold small piece of fabric in half lengthwise with right sides together. Sew along long side ½" in from edge. Trim seam and turn right side out. Fold in half and sew across edge (½" seam). Baste to top of one triangle piece on right side, with raw edges of strap to snipped top of triangle. Finish as for regular pillow.

Terrycloth Bolster

materials   1 piece of terrycloth 19" x 19"
2 circular pieces of terrycloth with 6½" diameters
Inner pad

Make up as for regular bolster using ½" seams.

Lounging Pillow

This pillow has its own "mat" attached to it. You just unroll it for use in the backyard or on the beach and simply roll it up again when you are through.

materials   2 pieces of sturdy fabric each 86" x 26"
Inner pad 12½" x 24½"

With right sides together, sew around two long sides and one short side, 1" from edges. Turn right side out and press. Measure down 13" from raw edges and stitch across fabric on the outside. Insert pad and slip stitch across top. If you prefer to use a burr type closing on this pillow, follow directions on page 32.

Crab Pillow

materials   2 pieces of fabric 13" x 13"
Scrap of fabric for crab

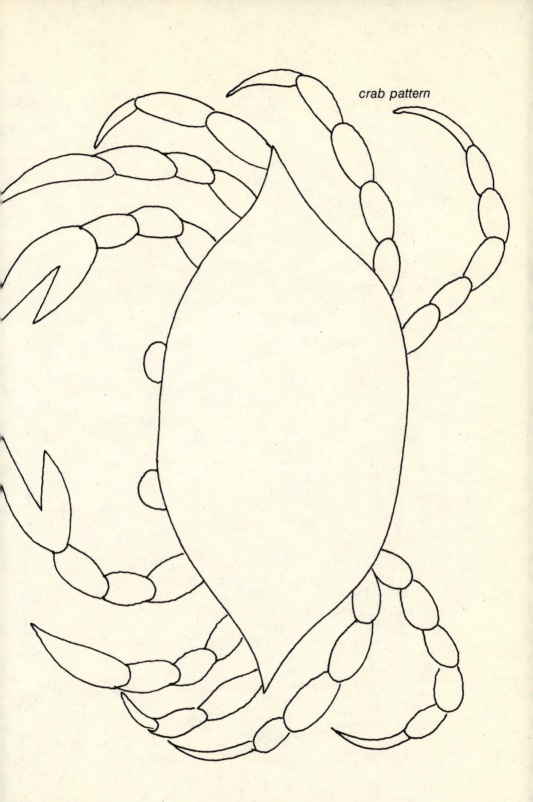

crab pattern

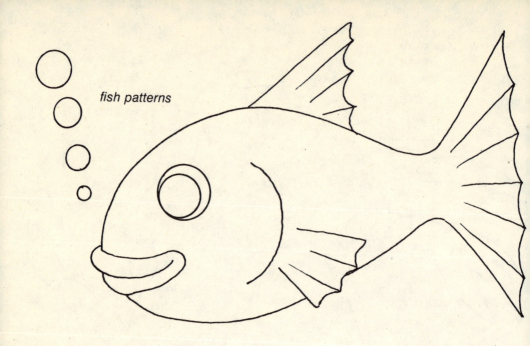

fish patterns

Embroidery thread for crab's eyes
Inner pad

 Enlarge pattern of crab if you wish, then cut out of scrap of fabric. Appliqué to front cover piece. Embroider eyes in satin stitch. Finish as for regular pillow. Crab may be embroidered instead of appliquéd.

Fish Pillow

materials

2 pieces of fabric 11" x 15"
Scraps of fabric for fish
Embroidery thread for eyes, mouth, fins,
 and bubbles
Inner pad

 Cut fish out of scraps of fabric. Appliqué to front cover piece, one in front of the other, about 1" from edges. Embroider eyes, mouth, and fins in satin stitch. Bubbles are worked in stem stitch. Finish as for regular pillow.

garden and patio pillows

19

Most people who have gardens do all their own weeding, trimming, and so on and usually have all the necessary equipment: forks, trowels, trimmers, electric this and that. But what do they kneel on? You guessed it, a scrap of cardboard, or old newspaper. Why not a nice soft, flat pillow made especially for this purpose? And, while we are at it, how about some lovely plump, comfy cushions for the garden chairs.

For this category choose your fabrics from the informal list. Pick the sturdier ones that wash well such as duck, denim, linen, and sailcloth.

Gay, bright colors and cheerful patterns make ideal garden pillows. Use any decoration you wish, but be reasonable. Don't use buttons on a pillow designed to be knelt on.

Since these pillows will be washed more often than others you may prefer to use a burr type closing for the cover instead of slip stitching it.

Here are eight ideas for garden pillows, but do

remember that these pillows are interchangeable with the informal ones.

Busy Bee Pillow

materials

2 pieces of fabric 17″ x 17″
Scrap of fabric for beehive
Embroidery thread in black, yellow, and white
Inner pad

   Enlarge pattern of hive and cut out of scrap of fabric. Appliqué to front cover piece (in center). Embroider detail on hive in black stem stitch. Work yellow and black bees in satin stitch, and wings in white stem stitch. Finish as for regular pillow.

busy bee patterns

Deck Chair Pillow

materials   2 pieces of fabric 11" x 15"
4 pieces of tape or ribbon each 10" long
Inner pad

Sew a piece of tape at top edge of cover piece 3" from end (right side of fabric). Repeat on left top side. Short edge of tape should be even with top edge of cover piece. Sew tape at both ends of each cover piece. Finish as for regular pillow.

Kneeling Pillow

materials   2 pieces of fabric 15" x 13"
2 pieces of fabric 7¼" x 4¼"
Inner pad
1 piece of fabric 57" x 3" for boxing (optional)

Appliqué small pieces of fabric onto larger one, 1" up from bottom and 2" in from edges. Finish as for regular plain or boxed pillow.

Apple Pillow

materials   2 octagonal pieces of fabric 13" across middle
Scraps of fabric for apple and leaves
1½ yds. of fringe
Inner pad

Enlarge pattern of apple and cut from scrap of fabric. Repeat this with leaf pattern. Appliqué apple and leaves onto cover piece. Baste fringe to right side of same piece. Finish as for regular pillow.

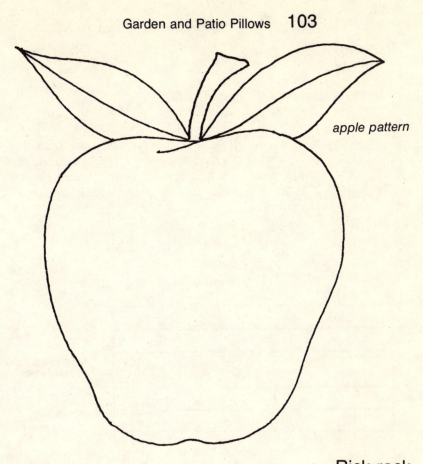

apple pattern

Rick-rack Pillow

materials

2 circular pieces of fabric with diameters of 13"
1 piece of fabric for frill 74" x 6"
1½ yds. wide rick-rack trim
Inner pad

Sew rick-rack around outside edge of cover piece on right side of fabric 2" in from edge. Sew another row 2" inside this one. Make up as for regular ruffled pillow using ½" seams.

Braided Pillow

materials 2 pieces of fabric 13" x 19"
2 yds. of 1" wide braid
Inner pad

Sew braid from top to bottom on both sides of front, 2½" in from ends. Sew another two pieces of braid, one at top and one at bottom of front piece, 2½" in from edges (see drawing). Make up as for regular pillow.

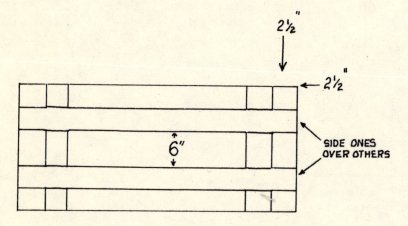

Frilled Half Moon

materials 1 piece of fabric (circular) 22" in diameter
1 piece of fabric for frill 114" x 6"
Inner pad

Fold circle in half and cut along fold. Fold frill piece in half, right sides together, and stitch across short ends. Turn right side out, fold in half crosswise with wrong sides together. Run two rows of basting stitch, ¼" apart, along raw edges. Gather to fit pillow cover. Finish as for ruffled pillow.

I have always been fascinated by the sea. Whenever our family went to the seaside for a day, I returned home loaded with "treasures"—assorted seashells, small bits of colored glass that had been smoothed by the action of sand and water, pebbles galore, and even seaweed. Maybe this is why I like the nautical look so much. It reminds me of the sea.

For these pillows, strong cotton, denim, sailcloth, duck, and felt are good choices of fabric and foam or kapok are ideal fillings.

Motifs such as anchors, life belts, flags, and so on can be appliquéd onto the covers of pillows. Sometimes you may find fabrics that are printed with nautical designs.

The square, rectangle, triangle, and circle are suitable shapes and those may be piped, boxed, flanged, or left plain.

Here are five ideas for pillows with that nautical look and I am sure you could think up more.

Anchor Pillow

materials   2 pieces of fabric 13" x 13"
Embroidery thread
Inner pad

Transfer the design, after enlarging it, onto front cover piece. Embroider in satin stitch and stem stitch. Make up cover as for regular pillow.

anchor pattern

Life Belt Pillow

materials   2 circular pieces of fabric with 13" diameters
1¼ yds. of piping
Embroidery thread
Inner pad

Transfer the design as shown. Embroider in satin and stem stitch. Make up cover as for regular piped pillow.

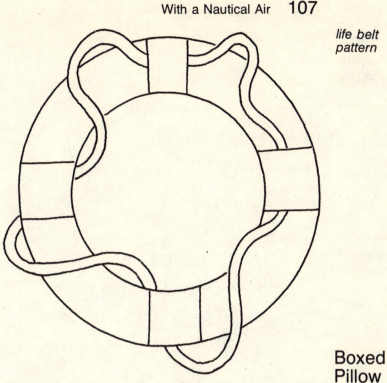

*life belt
pattern*

Boxed
Pillow

materials

2 pieces of fabric with nautical print 14″ x 20″
1 piece of plain fabric for boxing 69″ x 4″
Inner pad
   Make up as for regular boxed pillow using 1″
seams.

Striped
Pillow

materials

1 piece of fabric 15″ x 13″
2 pieces of red fabric 13″ x 3″
3 pieces of white fabric 13″ x 3″
2 pieces of blue fabric 13″ x 3″
1½ yds. piping
Inner pad
   Sew small pieces of fabric together with ½″
seams as follows: red, white, blue, white, blue,
white, red. Use as front cover piece and construct
pillow as for regular piped one.

Ship's Wheel Pillow

materials   2 pieces of fabric (circular) 13" diameters
Embroidery thread
1¼ yds. of piping
Inner pad

Enlarge and transfer design onto front cover piece. Embroider in satin and stem stitch. Finish as for regular piped pillow with ½" seams.

ship's wheel pattern

21

Giant pillows that can serve as seats, poufs, or cushions, are no harder to make than regular sizes, they just need more fabric and stuffing.

Giant pillows can be made out of informal, formal, or mod fabrics, it all depends on where the finished pillow will be placed and how it will be used. They can be constructed in any shape, simply increase the regular pattern size to the dimensions you need for your giant pillows.

Decorate these pillows the same way as others: fringed, ruffled, piped, buttoned, flanged, boxed; in fact, just about any way at all.

Use an inexpensive filling, since you will need a large amount. If you prefer a foam form, shop around a bit before you buy. I found a difference in price of $1.32 between pillow forms in two stores. (That's enough for another pillow!)

On the following pages are six ideas to start you off.

Fringed Circle Pillow

materials   2 circular pieces of fabric with 25″ diameters
2¼ yds. of 3″ wide fringe
4½ yds. of wide rick-rack
Inner pad
   Sew five rows of rick-rack across cover, 4″ apart and 5″ from each end. Baste fringe around outside of cover on right side of fabric. Finish as for regular fringed pillow.

Patchwork Pillow

materials   32 - 7″ x 7″ squares of fabric
                                      or
72 - 5″ x 5″ squares
4 pieces of fabric 30¼″ x 5″ for boxing
Inner pad
   Sew 16 (36) patches together for each cover piece using ½″ seams. Join boxing pieces together at short ends with 1″ seams. Make up as for regular boxed pillow using 1″ seams.

Pom-pom Fringed Square

materials   2 pieces of fabric 25″ x 25″
3 yds. of pom-pom fringe
Inner pad
   Construct as for regular pom-pom pillow.

Flanged Pillow

materials   2 pieces of octagonal-shaped fabric 30″ x 30″
                  across center

Inner pad

With right sides together sew around cover leaving opening. Sew 1" in from edge. Turn right side out and press. Sew around cover on outside 3" in from edge, leaving opening. Insert pad and sew across opening. Slip stitch flange opening.

Piped Square

materials

4 pieces of fabric 19" x 19"
8 yds. piping
2 - 1½" button forms
Scraps of fabric for buttons
Inner pad

Fold each piece of fabric in half to form triangle and cut along fold. Sew four triangles together to form a square inserting piping in seam of ½". Make up as for regular piped pillow. Cover buttons and attach one to center of each side.

Triangle Pillow

materials

2 triangular pieces of fabric 33" x 24" x 24"
2¼ yds. of pom-pom fringe
Inner pad

Make up a regular triangle pillow, then sew a row of pom-pom fringe around edge 2" in from sides.

patchwork pillows

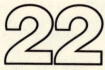

22

Patchwork is a very old craft, dating back many years. It can be simple or quite intricate.

It consists of sewing small patches of fabric together to form one big piece. The patches may be square, rectangular, triangular, octagonal, or a mixture of two or more!

There are a great many patterns that can be put together with patches. I worked up six lovely ones, however, that can be managed without difficulty.

Patches should be all the same fiber content; for example, all cotton, wool, or fur. They should also be all washable and colorfast or all dry cleanable. (If in doubt as to the colorfastness, wash a small piece of the fabric in question with a small piece of white or light fabric and observe the results. If it is not colorfast don't use it.) If you mix fibers you will have trouble later when you try to clean your pillows.

Patterned and solid color fabrics can be combined or used alone. This is a good way to use up any leftover material from other projects or pillows. Color will depend on what you have left over. You could make a many-colored pillow or use only a few colors. You might also choose a specific color and use solid and patterned fabric containing this color.

Patchwork pillows do not need any other decoration, although you might want to add a little rick-rack or embroidery for accent, or a plain ruffle. Both the front and back of the pillow may be patchwork, or you could have a plain back on the patchwork pillow. Boxed pillows look nice with patchwork fronts and backs and plain boxing fabric in between.

The square, rectangle, and boxed pillows are easiest to begin with, later you might like to try other shapes.

Here are instructions for six patchwork pillows.

Zodiac Pillow

materials

12 - 4" x 5" squares, solid colors
1 piece of fabric for back 12½" x 12½"
Embroidery thread in 12 different colors
Inner pad

Embroider a sign of the zodiac (see page 73) on each square, then sew the squares together using ½" seams. Place patchwork piece and back fabric right sides together and sew around three edges. Turn right side out, insert pad and sew up opening.

Rick-rack Patchwork

materials

16 - 4" x 4" squares, all different
1 piece of fabric for back 13" x 13"
3½ yds. of rick-rack trim (black or white)
Inner pad

Sew patches together using ½" seams. Sew

lengths of rick-rack across seams on right side of cover so that each patch is separated by it. On right side of one cover piece baste rick-rack around edges, ½" in from sides. Stitch front cover piece to back piece with right sides together using ½" seams. You may have to lift fabric every now and then to be sure you are sewing along the middle of the rick-rack. Turn right side out, insert pad and sew up opening. Rick-rack should form a stand-up edge on outside of pillow.

Diamond Patch Pillow

materials 16 - 4½" x 4½" squares in a solid color
16 - 4½" x 4½" squares of print fabric
1 piece of fabric for back 13" x 13"
Inner pad

Cut all squares in half from one corner to the other; this will make small triangles. Next, sew a solid triangle to a print one across base (long side). Sew squares together as shown in diagram. Use as front cover piece and make a regular square pillow.

diamond patch pattern

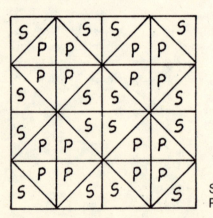

S = Solid
P = Print

materials

8 - 4" x 4" squares in a solid color
8 - 4" x 4" squares in a print fabric
1 piece of fabric for back 13" x 13"
Inner pad

Sew squares together as shown in diagram. Use ½" seams. Use as front cover piece and make up a regular square pillow.

plain patch pattern

P	S	S	P
S	P	P	S
S	P	P	S
P	S	S	P

Knitted Patchwork Pillow

See chapter 27, "Knitted Pillows."

Crocheted Patchwork Pillow

See chapter 28, "Crocheted Pillows."

appliqué pillows

Appliqué is another old craft. Designs and pictures are cut out of nonfraying fabric and sewn onto a background fabric.

Background fabric should be of a sturdy nature such as:

Linen	Felt	Duck
Denim	Burlap	Sailcloth

Any nonfraying fabric can be used for the appliqué designs, which, except for felt, are cut with an extra ¼" to ½" all around. This extra fabric is turned under and pressed to form a good edge. Designs are then positioned on the background and sewn. No extra fabric is needed when felt is used as it already has a good edge and will not fray. For this reason felt is ideal for appliqué work.

Designs can be sewn on by machine but most people sew them on by hand. The running stitch, blanket stitch, and overstitch are the most commonly used stitches. Some people **anchor** the design with white glue before stitching, others use pins. Use whichever method suits you best. Designs are sewn on before making up the cover.

All shapes can be appliquéd but plain fabric is better than a patterned fabric.

Any fabric scraps can be used for appliqué. It is a good idea, however, to stick to a single kind of fiber fabric in one pillow. This will eliminate problems at cleaning time.

Pictures and designs found in books and magazines can be enlarged or made smaller by the method described in chapter 25.

Below are patterns and instructions for eight appliquéd pillows.

Flowered Pillow

materials

2 pieces of fabric each 17" x 17"
Assorted flowers cut from floral patterned fabric
Inner pad

Appliqué flowers onto front cover piece, using overstitching. Leave 2½" plain all around cover. With right sides together, sew front section to back section around three sides. Use ½" seams. Turn right side out, then stitch around the same three sides on outside of cover, 2" in from edges. Insert pad and sew across fourth edge 2" in, then slip stitch outer edge.

Sunflower Pillow

materials

2 circular pieces of felt with diameters of 18"
1 piece of yellow 8" x 26"
1 piece of orange felt 7" x 26"
Orange embroidery silk
Inner pad

Cut out eight yellow petals and eight orange petals. Place orange petals side by side to form circle in center of front cover piece. Stitch lower half of petals only. Arrange yellow petals between orange ones, then stitch around entire petal with overstitching. Cut out orange center and stitch to the middle of flower, using overstitches. Now sew front section of cover to back section with right sides together, leaving opening. Turn right side out, insert pad, and sew up opening.

sunflower pattern

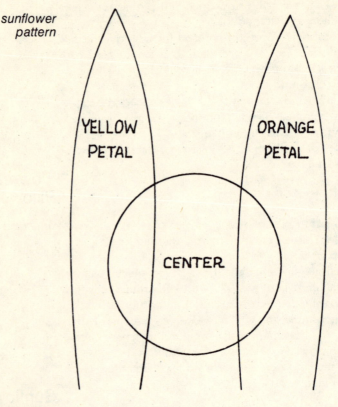

YELLOW PETAL

ORANGE PETAL

CENTER

Butterfly Pillow

materials 2 pieces of fabric 13" x 17"
1 piece of fabric 11" x 13" for wings
Small piece of black fabric for body
Small scrap of fabric for circles
Embroidery thread
Inner pad

Cut out wings and body and appliqué onto front of cover piece. Use overstitching. Embroider lines and circles on wings. Use stem stitch for lines and satin stitch for circles. "Feelers" on head are embroidered in stem stitch. Finish as for regular pillow.

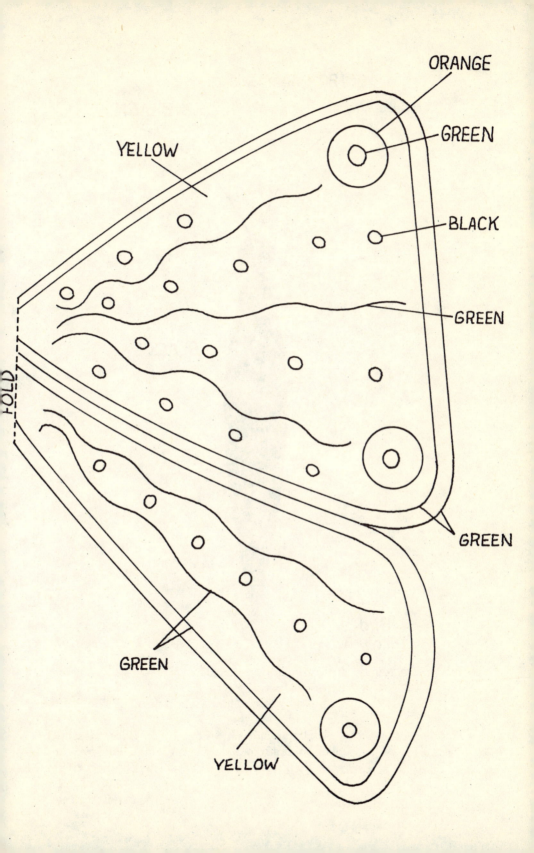

ORANGE

GREEN

YELLOW

BLACK

GREEN

FOLD

GREEN

GREEN

YELLOW

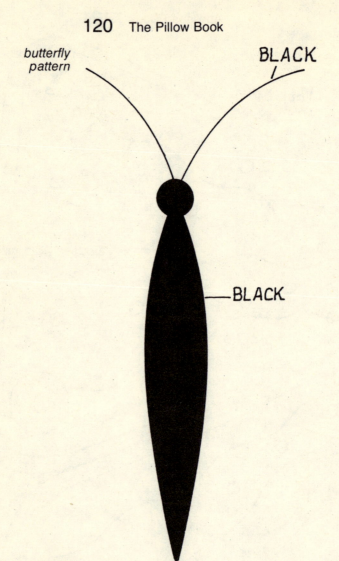

butterfly pattern

BLACK

BLACK

Bird Pillow

materials 2 pieces of fabric each 9" x 13"
Scraps of fabric for bird
Embroidery thread for nest and detail on bird
Inner pad

Appliqué bird onto front cover piece. Use stem stitch to embroider details on wings, tail, eye, and legs. Beak is done in satin stitch. The nest is em-

broidered in straight stitch and the eggs in satin
stitch. Finish as for regular pillow.

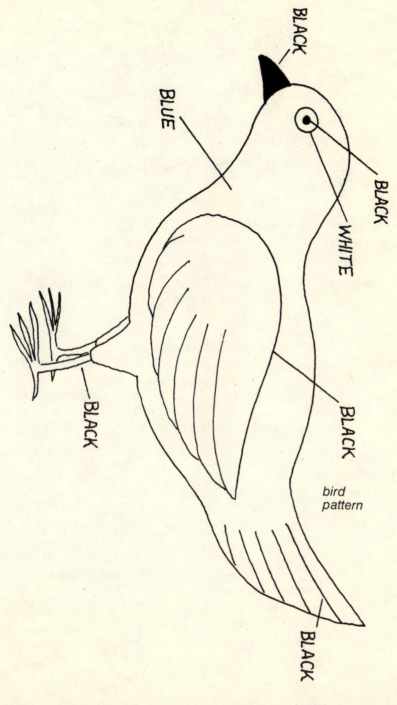

bird
pattern

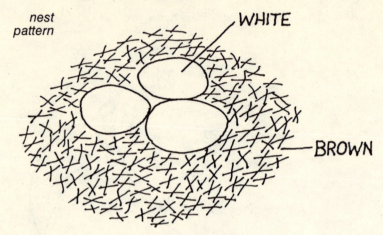

nest pattern

WHITE

BROWN

Circles on Circle Pillow

materials   2 circular pieces of fabric with 13" diameters
Scraps of fabric for circles
Embroidery thread
Inner pad

Cut out 19 circles with 2" diameters from the scraps of fabric. Arrange 10 circles around outside cf front cover piece, overstitch into place. Arrange eight circles inside of previous circle with sides overlapping slightly, overstitch into place. Stitch one circle in center. Finish as for regular pillow.

Woodland Pillow

materials   2 pieces of fabric each 10" x 14"
Scraps of fabric or felt for toadstools and grass
Embroidery thread or yarn for leaves and snail
Inner pad

Cut out toadstools and grass, arrange on front cover piece as shown in color plate III, overstitch in place. Embroider leaves in satin stitch and stem in stem stitch. Snail is couched-shell and satin-stitched body, the eyes are straight stitches. Finish cover as for regular pillow.

*woodland
motifs*

Persian Pillow

materials   2 pieces of solid colored fabric, size as desired
2 strips cut from fabric with a Persian design
· Inner pad
Place the strips at right angles to each other 2"
in from edge and sew onto front cover piece. Finish
as for regular pillow.

Mod Pillow

materials   2 pieces of solid black fabric, size as desired
2 strips, width as desired, cut from a bold
black-and-white patterned fabric
Inner pad
Place the two strips parallel onto the front cover
piece. Arrange for equal spacing, and appliqué.
Finish as for regular pillow.

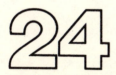

Needlepoint consists of stitches worked on a canvas. The canvas has so many holes to the inch. A blunt needle and tapestry yarn is used to embroider stitches and patterns on the canvas.

Canvas may be single mesh—mono canvas, or double mesh—Penelope canvas.

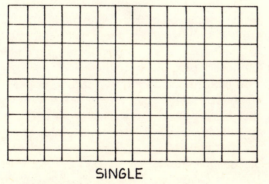

SINGLE

canvas

It may have from three to 24 or more holes to the inch. Canvas with three to five holes per inch is known as quick point canvas. Petit point is the name given to canvas with 24 holes to the inch.

DOUBLE

yarns   Almost any yarn can be used but there are special needlepoint yarns available. These yarns have a tighter twist and are strong enough to stand up under the wear and tear of being pulled through canvas. I have used double knit yarn, however, with no trouble, by keeping the working yarn short —no longer than 15".

needles   The needles used in needlepoint have large eyes to accommodate yarn and blunt tips so as not to damage the canvas. They are bought under the name of **tapestry needles,** and each package contains different sizes: from small ones for petit point to larger ones for quick point. Ordinary needles are of no use in this type of work.

transferring designs   Designs can be transferred onto canvas with ink, pencil, paint, or carbon paper. (Felt marker pens are handy here.) Trace the design onto the canvas by placing canvas over design and drawing around the lines that show through.

Another method is to use carbon paper. Place it on canvas with design on top of it and anchor with sticky tape. Then draw over design with a pencil or knitting needle. Go over the faint lines on the canvas with a felt marker. You could also draw designs free-hand.

preparing canvas   When preparing the canvas, allow enough canvas for design, background, an extra two or three rows of background work all around, and 1" to 2" of unworked canvas all around. Measure and cut canvas to desired size.

Bind edges of canvas with strong masking tape. This will prevent edges from fraying and stop yarn from catching on them. Canvas can then be rolled up or around a tube for carrying and unrolled to be worked.

If you plan on doing a lot of needlepoint, it may be worthwhile to buy a needlepoint frame. Canvas is unrolled onto frame which rests on the floor. A frame leaves both hands free to do the needlepoint.

estimating yarn

To estimate the amount of yarn required for needlepoint, find out how much yarn it takes to cover 1 sq. in. Multiply this by the total number of square inches in the needlepoint piece. Divide by 36 to get the number of yards of wool you will need to cover the canvas.

If you have a design on a background total up the number of square inches in the design and subtract this number from the total amount of square inches in the whole canvas.

pressing

Finished piece should be pressed face down with a warm iron and a damp cloth.

blocking

Sometimes stitching will have pulled the canvas out of shape. If this happened you will have to block the canvas.

Dampen and stretch the canvas to correct measurements. Then anchor around the edges with push pins or tacks every inch or so and leave to dry.

making up pillow

To make up the pillow, cut a back cover piece out of velvet, velveteen, corduroy, or some other firm fabric. When sewing cover, stitch inside two or three rows of needlepoint. Slice off corners before turning right side out. Finish as for regular pillow.

Needlepoint Stitches

Do not have your yarn any longer than 18" to 20". Begin by taking a few running stitches at the side or back of canvas and finish the same way.

Continental stitch

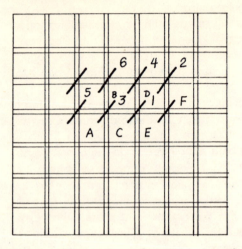

Bring needle up through point 1, then down through point 2, up through point 3, down through 4, and so on. To return bring needle up through point A, down through point B, up through C, down through D, and so on.

Cross stitch

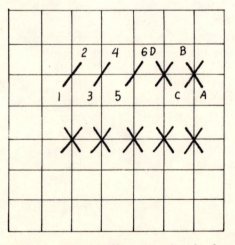

Make a row of half crosses first by bringing needle up through point 1, then down through point 2, up through point 3, down through point 4. To work return row bring needle up through point A, down through point B, up through C, down through D, and so on.

Although there are many needlepoint stitches, I have used only these two simple ones for the pillows in this chapter.

materials

4 ozs. of yellow rug yarn
4 ozs. of white rug yarn
Piece of canvas (4 holes to the inch) 14" x 18"
Piece of velveteen 13" x 17"
Inner pad

After marking off an area 12" x 16" on canvas, follow diagram for design using all cross stitches.

pattern

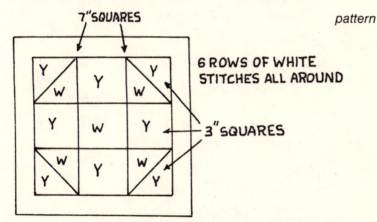

Using velveteen as back of cover, make up pillow.

materials

8 ozs. of rug yarn in four different colors
Piece of canvas (4 holes to the inch) 13½" x 13½"
Piece of velveteen 13" x 13"
Inner pad

Mark off a 12" x 12" area on canvas and divide into 3" x 3" squares. Work each square in a different color using cross stitch. Make up pillow with velveteen as back of cover.

Red, White, and Blue Pillow

materials 4 ozs. red rug yarn
2 ozs. white rug yarn
2 ozs. blue rug yarn
Piece of canvas (4 holes to the inch) 13½" x 13½"
Piece of velveteen 13" x 13"
Inner pad

Mark off a 12" x 12" area on canvas and divide in half from left bottom corner to right top corner. Divide one of the triangles in half. Cross stitch large triangle in red yarn, one small triangle in blue yarn, and the other one in white. Make up pillow with velveteen as back of cover.

pattern

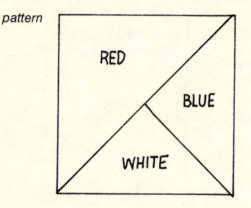

Triangle Pillow

materials 4 ozs. of pink double knit yarn
4 ozs. of purple double knit yarn
Piece of canvas (10 holes to the inch) 14" x 18"
Piece of velveteen 13" x 17"
Inner pad

Mark off an area 12" x 16" on canvas. Divide area from corners to corners (making four triangles). Work top and bottom triangles in pink yarn, the right and left triangles in purple yarn. Use continental stitch. This piece of needlepoint will need blocking. After doing this it can be made into a pillow cover with a velveteen backing.

materials

4 ozs. of dark green rug yarn
6 ozs. of light green rug yarn
Piece of canvas (4 holes to the inch) 15" x 15"
Piece of velveteen 14" x 14"
Inner pad
   Mark off a 13" x 13" area on canvas. Using cross stitch, follow diagram for design.

pattern

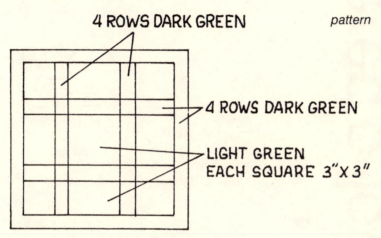

4 ROWS DARK GREEN

4 ROWS DARK GREEN

**LIGHT GREEN
EACH SQUARE 3"X 3"**

Make up pillow with velveteen backing.

embroidered pillows

The art of decorative stitching on fabric is known as embroidery. It is used on clothing, household linens, wall hangings, pillows, and so on to make them more attractive or to add interest.

Just about any fabric will take embroidery, for example:

Linen	Cotton	Sailcloth
Denim	Gingham	Burlap
Felt	Indianhead	Wool

Different yarns are used on certain types of fabrics. On fine cottons and gingham, embroidery silk is used. This silk is made up of six strands and from one to six strands can be used depending on just how delicate the fabric is. On linen, sailcloth, felt, or denim, heavier yarn or crewel wool should be used. Heavy yarns can also be split or separated to form finer yarns.

needles   Needles come in different sizes and numbers. The larger the number, the finer the needle. Choose fine needles for fine fabrics and larger needles for heavier fabrics. There is also a crewel needle for working with crewel wool.

You will find embroidery a lot easier to do if you work with a hoop. This keeps the fabric taut and even, so that stitches can be made neatly and regular. The hoop consists of two rings, one larger than the other, and is held in the hand. Fabric is positioned over the smaller ring then the larger ring is placed over it and pressed down. Some hoops are tightened by a small screw.

hoops and frames

A frame is actually an oversized hoop on a stand. It leaves the hands free for embroidery. It comes in table or floor models.

Designs

You can purchase fabrics with designs already stamped on them or you can buy commercial transfers and stamp your own fabric. But occasionally, in a book or magazine, you come across a design or picture that you would like to use as a pattern for embroidery. What you do is trace the design onto a piece of paper, and then beg, borrow, or buy some dressmaker's carbon paper. Place carbon face down on fabric, put tracing on top, and anchor with sticky tape. Draw over the design using a blunt point such as a knitting needle or dressmaker's tracing wheel.

You can use patterned fabric and embroider the design on it using the same color yarns as on the fabric. If you allow yourself to be carried away doing this you can end up with some very lovely pillows.

If you wish to enlarge a design, measure and mark every ½" across top, bottom, and sides of design. Connect marks from top to bottom and side to side. You now have a series of ½" squares. Draw larger squares on a separate piece of paper, then copy the lines of the design in the small squares into the corresponding larger squares. You can make a design smaller by simply reversing this procedure.

enlarging designs

Embroidery Stitches

Your thread should be no longer than 18″, or it may become tangled or knotted. Begin by taking two or three small running stitches at the back of your work and finish the same way. Here again I have included only the stitches used on the pillows in this chapter, although there are dozens more.

Running stitch

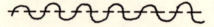

Needle is pulled through at point 1, pushed in at point 2, out at 3, in at 4, and so on. Stitches may be even or uneven (as for instance, two short and one long).

Whipped running stitch

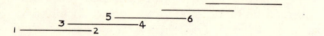

Thread is woven in and out of running stitch.

Stem stitch

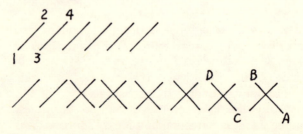

Needle is pulled through at point 1, pushed in at point 2, out at 3, in at 4, out at 5. This stitch is often used for stems and outlines.

Cross stitch

One row of half cross stitch is worked first, then a second row to complete crosses. Pull needle through at point 1, push back in at point 2, out at 3, in at 4, and so on to end of design. Second row starts by pulling thread through at point A, in at point B, out at C, and in at D.

Backstitch

Pull needle out at point 1, push in at point 2, pull out at point 3, in again at 2, out at 4, in at 3, out at 5. Also used for stems and outline.

Seed stitch

A collection of tiny straight stitches going in all directions. Used as filling-in or centers of flowers.

Straight stitch

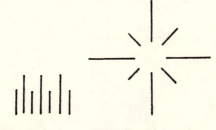

Simply a straight stitch in various lengths, sometimes used for flowers.

Couching

Overstitches used at regular intervals to hold a length of yarn in place. Yarn can be made into designs such as flowers and animals. Designs are drawn on fabric first, and sometimes white glue is used to anchor yarn in place before it is couched.

Satin stitch

A series of straight stitches used for filling in on such things as petals and leaves. Can be worked side to side or up and down. Stitches are kept even at edges of design.

Overstitch

Small stitches taken over the top of edges. Also used for couching and appliqué work.

Blanket stitch

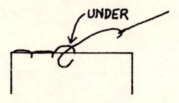

Similar to overstitch except needle is passed through loop of stitch before going on to another.

to make up   Embroider cover piece before making up into case for pillow. Place face down on a padded surface and press with a warm iron. Use as regular cover piece. Pillows may be fringed, ruffled, piped, or boxed.

On the following pages are designs for six embroidered pillows.

2 pieces of fabric 13″ x 17″
Black embroidery thread
Inner pad

   Transfer motifs to cover piece. Use as many as you like to cover fabric. Embroider in black satin stitch and stem stitch. Finish as for regular pillow.

Music Motif Pillow

music motifs

2 pieces of fabric 13″ x 13″
Embroidery thread
Inner pad

   Embroider "stars" all over pillow then make up as for regular cover.

Star Pillow

stars

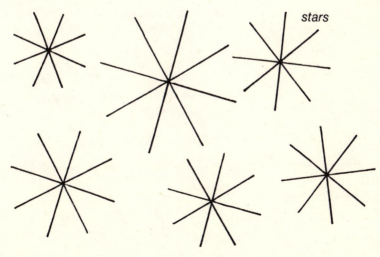

**Diamond
Motif
Pillow**

2 pieces of fabric 13" x 17"
Inner pad
Embroidery thread or crewel wool

   Transfer diamonds to cover piece, an equal distance apart (1"). Embroider diamonds in a variety of stitches. Make up cover as for regular pillow.

*diamond
motif*

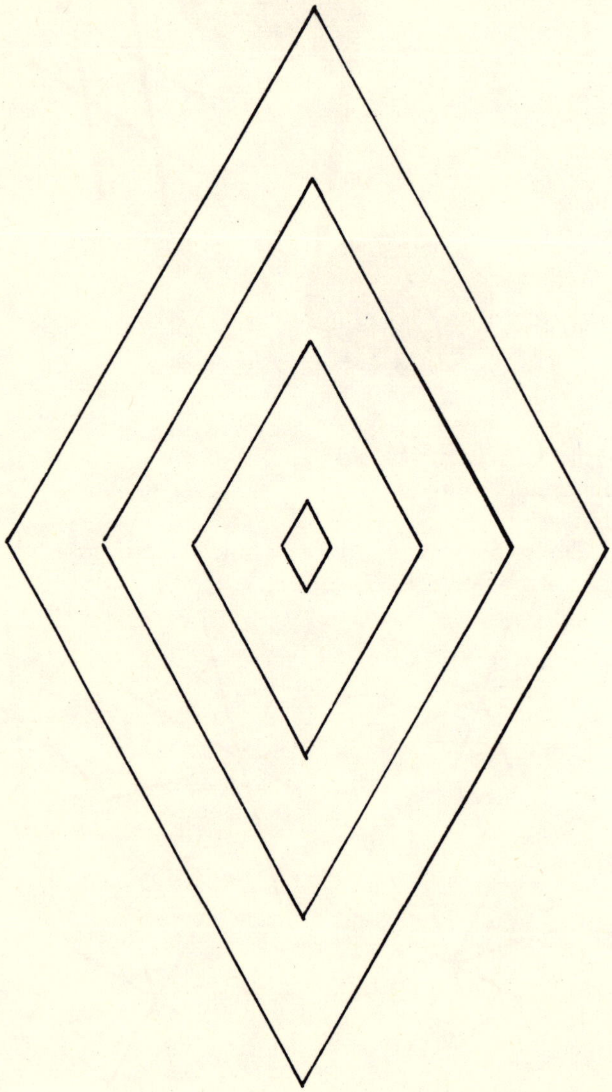

plate I

Crocheted pillows are almost certain to captivate. Shown here clockwise (starting at upper left) are: Mauve and Purple Pillow, Hexagon Pillow, Spider Web Pillow, Spotted White Pillow, Red Triangle, Blue-Striped Fringed Pillow, and Bolster.

plate II
Children, teens, and grown-ups alike enjoy novelty pillows. Make your own Funny Face and Strawberry Pillows for fun or gift-giving.

plate III
Use your handicraft—needlepoint, embroidery, appliqué—to add that special something to traditional square or rectangular pillows.

plate IV
Strips of fabric or trim appliquéd to solid fabric pillows give a delightful effect.

plate V
Get a feel
for texture.
Use
corduroy,
velvet, fur,
and linen
for simply
elegant
pillows.

plate VI
A silk-textured gold
bolster is lovely, but if
eye-catching appeal is
wanted try a favorite
printed fabric.

plate VII

Never underestimate the versatility of knitted patterns. The
lovely pillows shown here clockwise (starting at the top) are:
Crocheted Edge Triangle, Gold Moss Stitch Pillow, Blue Cable
Pillow, Purple Ribbed Pillow, Striped Pillow, Spotted Pillow, with
Green Trellis Pillow in the center.

2 pieces of fabric 13″ x 15″
Embroidery thread in brown, blue
1½ yds. of piping
Inner pad

Transfer seahorse pattern to front cover piece. Embroider in brown stem stitch. Work blue stem stitch waves around seahorses. Make up as for regular piped pillow.

Seahorse Pillow

seahorses

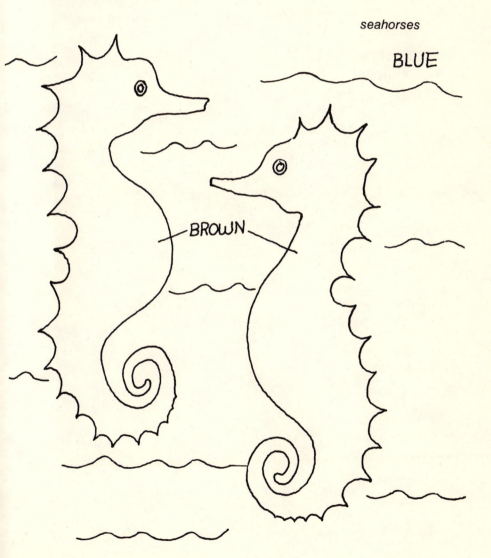

BLUE

BROWN

Floral Pillow

materials   2 octagonal pieces of floral patterned fabric
    13" across center
Embroidery thread in the colors on the fabric
1½ yds. of fringe
Inner pad

Embroider flowers on fabric in a variety of stitches. Make up as for regular fringed pillow.

Patchwork Pillow

materials   8 - 4" x 4" patterned squares
8 - 4" x 4" plain squares
1½ yds. of piping
Embroidery thread to match design on fabric
Inner pad

Embroider designs on patterned squares, then sew together with plain ones, alternating one patterned and one plain. Use ½" seams. Make up as for regular piped pillow.

26

The type of smocking used for these pillows is called honeycomb smocking. Small amounts of fabric are caught with the needle, then stitched to form little honeycombs, as shown.

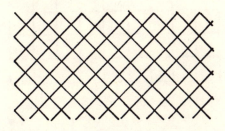

the fabric

Checked and striped fabrics are easy to work with because they are already marked. Plain fabric has to be marked first with a series of dots before one can begin to smock.

I picked checked fabric not only because it is easy to smock (or because it is my favorite), but because it makes such attractive pillows. The colors are lovely and the cushions can be made in so many different ways.

For smocked pillows buy wash and wear fabric as it does not wrinkle and crush while you are working with it. The pillows in this chapter were all smocked on 1″ size check, but you can experiment with different sizes.

The square, rectangle, and bolster are the easiest shapes to smock, and they may be piped, ruffled, or left plain.

yarn Embroidery silk, three or six strands, was used for these pillows.

needles Use fine embroidery needles for this type of work.

Smocking

To do smocking, bring the needle through from behind to front of work at corner of square, point 1. Move to opposite corner, point 2, and pick up a small amount (pinhead size) of fabric. Pull gently so that corners come together, then take a small stitch to secure and push needle through to back of work. Bring out at point 3, connect to point 4 as above. Bring needle out at point 5, connect to point 6. Then go to point 7, connect to point 8, then to point 9 and connect to point 10 and so on to end of row.

Start back at top and work down, repeat this until all fabric has been smocked. Be sure, however, to leave thread loose at back of work or puckers will form.

Leave 1" all around piece unworked.

There are literally dozens of color combinations that will yield lovely smocked pillows, but here are a few you might like to try:

try these combinations

Color of Check with White	Color of Thread	Color of Backing
Pink	Red	Red
Yellow	Brown	Brown
Black	Black	Black
Green	Dark green	Dark green
Aqua	Navy	Navy
Orange	Brown	Brown
Yellow	Green	Green
Blue	Navy	Navy
Red	Maroon	Maroon
Pink	Maroon	Maroon
Yellow	Orange	Orange
Yellow	Blue	Blue
Green	Blue	Blue
Pink	Green	Green
Aqua	Turquoise	Turquoise
Yellow	Purple	Purple
Pink	Brown	Brown
Blue	Red	Red
Any	Black	Black

1 piece of velveteen (aqua) 19" x 23"
1 piece of gingham (aqua, 1" checks) 19" x 46"
2 skeins of turquoise embroidery silk
Inner pad

Giant Aqua Pillow

Using three strands of silk, smock gingham piece, leaving 1" all around unsmocked. Use as regular cover piece and finish cover using velveteen for the back.

1 piece of cotton (purple) 15" x 15"
1 piece of gingham (purple, 1" checks) 15" x 30"
Purple embroidery silk
2 yds. purple piping

Purple Piped Square

Inner pad
    Using three stands of silk, smock gingham piece. Use as cover piece and make a piped pillow.

Green Paneled Pillow

1 piece of cotton (green) 17" x 19"
2 pieces of cotton (green) 7" x 17"
1 piece of gingham (green, 1" checks) 14" x 17"
Dark green embroidery silk
Inner pad
    Using three strands of silk, smock gingham piece as for giant pillow. Sew one small piece of green cotton to both sides of smocked piece (seams on the inside). Make up pillow using large green piece of cotton for back of cover.

Orange Inside-out Pillow

1 piece of cotton (brown) 15" x 15"
1 piece of gingham (orange, 1" checks) 15" x 30"
Orange embroidery silk
Inner pad
    Smock gingham piece as usual but instead of carrying thread at back of work, leave it at the front (smocked piece is turned inside-out leaving the opposite side of smocking as the front of the pillow). Make up as for regular pillow.

Pink Bolster

2 pieces of cotton (pink) 6" x 19"
2 circular pieces of cotton (pink) with 6½" diameters
1 piece of gingham (pink, 1" checks) 17" x 19"
Pink embroidery silk
Inner pad
    Smock gingham piece using three strands of silk. Sew one piece of cotton (6" x 19") to each long side of smocked piece (½" seams). Fold in half with right sides together and stitch a few inches at both ends on botton (leave middle open). Sew end pieces to body piece using ½" seams. Finish as for regular bolster.

27

knitted pillows

No other pillow gives more of a feeling of warmth, care, and comfort than a well-made knitted pillow. And, happily, the variety of stitch patterns available allow a needlecrafter to create the **perfect** pillow for any home—to decoratively accent a Park Avenue parlor or see practical use in a rustic mountain cabin.

So that those of you who have never tried to knit won't have to miss out on the pillows in this chapter, and the enjoyment and satisfaction that knitting brings, we have included step-by-step instruction on how to knit, accompanied by clear and simple drawings. Basic knitting is quite easy to learn, and once you are comfortable with the knit and purl stitches you should have no trouble following the simple patterns for making the Purple Ribbed Pillow or the Gold Moss Stitch Pillow. The other six patterns given take a little more care and expertise, but they too can be done easily and in time to catch an admiring glance from your next visitor.

let's learn

Knitting Instructions

casting on To cast on:

1. Make a slip knot in the end of yarn. Slip loop onto left hand needle.

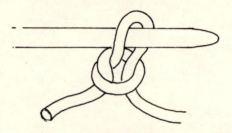

2. Insert right hand needle in front of loop with point of needle away from you. Wind yarn under and around point of right hand needle.

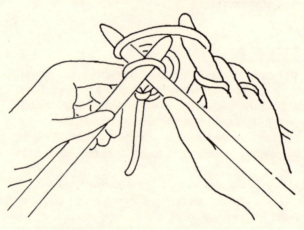

3. Draw a loop through.

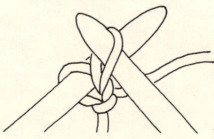

4. Slip the loop onto the left hand needle.

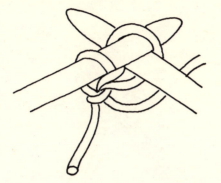

Repeat instructions 2 through 4 inserting right hand needle **between** the two stitches on left hand needle until you have the required amount of stitches on the left needle. This is known as the cable method of casting on.

To do the knit stitch: *knit*
1. Hold the needle with the stitches in your left hand. Have the yarn at the **back** of your work.
2. Insert right hand needle through front of the first stitch on the left needle (as you did in casting on) and wind the yarn under and around point of right needle.

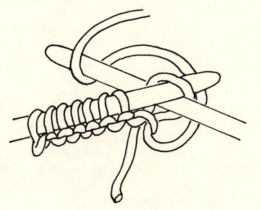

3. Pull a loop through.

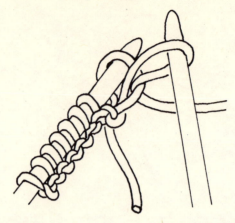

4. Slide stitch off of left needle.

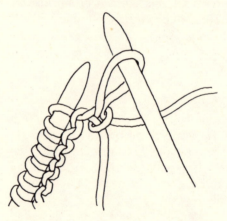

Repeat along row or until required number of stitches have been worked, or row has been knit.

purl   To do the purl stitch:
1. Hold the needle with the stitches in your left hand. Have yarn at the **front** of your work.
2. Insert right hand needle into front of stitch from point end of left needle (point of right needle should be **toward** you this time).

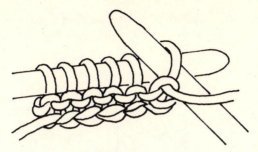

3. Wind yarn over and under point of needle.

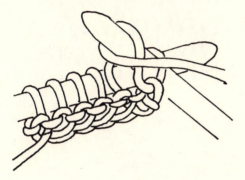

4. Draw loop through and slide stitch off of left needle.

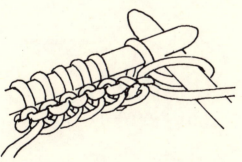

Repeat until the required number of stitches have been worked or row has been purled.

To cast or bind off: *casting off*
1. Knit or purl (or rib) two stitches from the left hand needle.

2. Slip the first stitch worked over the second (with the point of the left needle), and off the right needle.

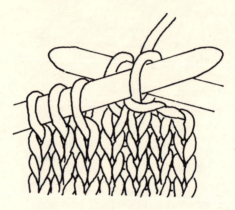

3. Work another stitch from the left needle.
4. Slip the previously worked stitch off the right needle as before.

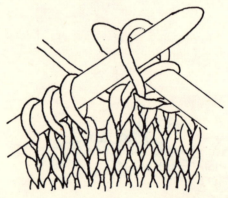

Continue along row until all stitches have been worked off of the left needle and only one remains on the right needle. Then cut yarn and pull through remaining stitch to fasten off.

decrease   To decrease:
1. Simply knit or purl two stitches together.

**Stitch
Names**

Knitting every row produces the garter stitch.

Knitting one row and purling one row, alternately, produces the stocking or stockinette stitch.

Knitting one stitch and purling one stitch, alternately, produces either the rib stitch, or the moss or rice stitch. (In working each row, if knit stitches are knitted and purl stitches are purled you will get a ribbed effect. When knit stitches are purled and purl stitches are knitted, the moss stitch is produced.)

**Knitting
Tips**

Before you go on, read the following carefully. Attention to details now will prevent problems from cropping up later on.

1. Read the pattern through from beginning to end once or twice to make certain you understand it.
2. Purchase enough yarn in the same dye lot to complete your pillow or you may be disappointed when you return to the store and find that they don't have any left. I usually buy 1 or 2 ozs. extra to be sure I have enough; whatever is left over I use for patches, embroidery, or toys.
3. Check your tension against that of the pattern by knitting a small 3" x 3" square. Count the number of stitches to 1". If you find you have too many, use needles one or two sizes larger, if you have too few stitches try needles one or two sizes smaller. These little patches can be made into a pillow later. If you go ahead and knit regardless of tension, you may run out of wool before your pillow is finished and the size of the pillow will suffer.
4. Join in a new ball of wool at the beginning of a row, never in the middle. You can be sure you have enough wool to finish a row by measuring it. Four times the length of the row should be plenty.
5. Do not jab the needles through your work or

the ball of wool when you put them away. This weakens and splits the fibers.

6. Keep the ball of wool in a small plastic bag with an elastic band slipped loosely around the top. This will keep your wool clean and free of tangles. Pull out wool as you need it.
7. Use a crochet hook to pick up dropped stitches.
8. Buy an inexpensive row marker that fits on the end of your needle. This makes counting rows easier.
9. Read list of abbreviations before starting.

yarns and needles Craft or double knit yarn was used for all patterns, and I used English size knitting needles to work each one. The needle sizes given, however, are the American sizes. (If you have or want to use English sized needles as I did, #8 American is the same as #5 English, and #6 American converts to #7 English.) Check with the sales person at the yarn shop if you are doubtful about the needles they carry. Most shops have a conversion chart handy.

blocking Blocking and pressing are quite simple. Gently stretch work out on a padded surface to the correct measurement. Secure every inch or so with a pin and press very lightly with a warm iron. Do not press ribbed surfaces.

Separate strands of craft or double knit wool or use three-ply wool in the same shade to sew up pillow pieces. Use loose backstitch or overstitch.

abbreviations Here is a list of the abbreviations used in the knit patterns given in this book:

k	knit	tog	together
p	purl	st(s)	stitch(es)
st st	stocking stitch– one row knit, one row purl	foll	following
		cont	continue
rep	repeat	c 6 f	cable six forward –slip the next three sts onto a cable needle, leave at front of work, knit the next three sts off left hand needle, then knit the three off of the cable needle
beg	beginning		
alt	alternate		
patt	pattern		
inc	increase		
dec	decrease		
rem	remaining		

**Purple
Ribbed
Pillow**
materials

6 ozs. of craft yarn
Pair of #8 knitting needles
Square inner pad
   Measurements: 12" x 12"—slightly stretched
   Tension: 3½ sts to 1"

Front and back alike (make two)   *pattern*

Cast on 42 sts.
Row 1:   K 2, p 2.
Row 2:   P 2, k 2.
Rep these two rows for k 2, p 2 rib till work measures
   12".
Cast off.

   Sew along three sides, insert pad, and sew up   *to make up*
opening. Make four tassels as described on p. 32.
Sew one tassel to each corner of pillow.

**Gold
Moss Stitch
Pillow**
materials

10 ozs. of craft yarn
Pair of #8 knitting needles
Large crochet hook
Inner pad
   Measurements: 16" x 10"
   Tension: 3 sts to 1"

Front and back alike (make two)   *pattern*

Cast on 48 sts.
Row 1:   K 1, p 1.
Row 2:   P 1, k 1.
Rep these two rows till work measures 10".
Cast off.

   Sew along three sides, insert pad, sew up open-   *to make up*
ing. Make fringe as follows:

Striped Pillow

materials 6 ozs. of double knit yarn in dark color
4 ozs. of double knit yarn in light color
Pair of #6 knitting needles
#4.50 international size crochet hook
Inner pad
Measurements: 13" x 13"
Tension: 5 sts to 1"

pattern **Front and back alike (make two)**
Cast on 65 sts in light wool.
Work in st st for 1". Join in dark wool and work 1"
in same stitch. Cont working in st st and alternate
colors in stripes of 1" till work measures 13".
Cast off.

to make up With right sides together sew around three edges,
turn right side out, insert pad, and sew up opening.

edging With dark wool work one row single crochet edging around pillow, then one row of double crochet
all around.

Spotted Pillow

materials 6 ozs. of double knit yarn in yellow
2 ozs. of double knit yarn in brown
Pair of #6 knitting needles
Inner pad
Measurements: 15" x 12"
Tension: 5 sts to 1"

pattern **Front and back alike (make two)**
With Y cast on 74 sts.

Y = Yellow
B = Brown

Row 1: K.
Row 2: P.
Row 3: K 3 Y, k 2 B, * k 4 Y, k 2 B, rep from * to
last 3 sts, k 3 Y.
Row 4: * p 2 Y, p 4 B, rep from * to last 2 sts, p 2 Y.
Row 5: * k 2 Y, k 4 B, rep from * to last 2 sts, k 2 Y.
Row 6: P 3 Y, p 2 B, * p 4 Y, p 2 B, rep from * to
last 3 sts, p 3 Y.

Row 7: K Y.

Row 8: P Y.

Row 9: K 6 Y, k 2 B, * k 4 Y, k 2 B, rep from * to
    last 6 sts, k 6 Y.

Row 10: P 5 Y, p 4 B, * p 2 Y, p 4 B, rep from * to
    last 5 sts, p 5 Y.

Row 11: K 5 Y, k 4 B, * k 2 Y, k 4 B, rep from * to
    last 5 sts, k 5 Y.

Row 12: P 6 Y, p 2 B, * p 4 Y, p 2 B, rep from * to
    last 6 sts, p 6 Y.

These 12 rows form pattern. Repeat pattern five
    times more, then first two rows once.

Cast off.

to make up

Block and press. With right sides together, sew
along three edges, then insert pad, sew up opening.

Patchwork Pillow

materials

8 ozs. of double knit yarn in eight different colors

Pair of #6 knitting needles

Inner pad

Measurements: 12" x 12"

Tension: 5 sts to 1"

pattern

Front and back alike (make two)

Work 16-3" x 3" squares for front, 16 for back.

For example: 4 moss stitch
          4 st st
          4 rib
          4 trellis
          or:
     16 all st st

to make up

Arrange squares in different patterns before you
sew them. When you have found the combination
you like most sew the squares together in that
formation.

Sew front piece to back piece with right sides
together, along three edges. Turn right side out,
insert pad, and sew up opening. If you wish you
may add a crochet or fringe edging around pillow.

crocheted pillows

Crocheting is very in at the moment, and it is quite easy to do. You use only one hook and about five different stitches. Although knitting consists of only two basic stitches while crocheting uses more, many people feel that it is much easier to learn to crochet, and quicker to do. Once you are able to work the crochet stitches smoothly you should be able to make a small crocheted pillow in a day. So even if you have never tried to crochet, pick up a needle (you'll need one to catch dropped knitted stitches anyway) and try learning the chain, slip stitch, and crochets. Soon you'll have dozens of hand-crocheted pillows to attest to your prowess.

Crocheting Instructions

chain   To work the chain:
1. Make a slip knot in the end of the yarn.
2. Slip loop onto crochet hook.

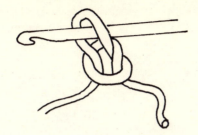

3. Wind yarn over hook and draw through loop on hook.

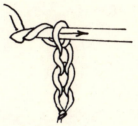

Continue this way until you have the number of chain stitches required for the pattern. The loop on the hook is not counted as a stitch.

To join rounds with the slip stitch:

slip stitch

1. Insert hook in first chain made.
2. Wind yarn around hook.

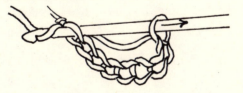

3. Draw yarn through both loops on hook.

To single crochet:

single crochet

1. Miss first chain from hook and insert hook between the two loops of the next chain.

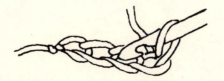

2. Wind yarn over hook and draw a loop through.
3. Yarn over hook and draw through both loops on hook.

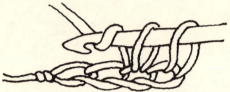

double crochet

To double crochet:

1. Wind yarn over hook.
2. Miss the first three chains from hook. Insert hook between the two loops of next chain.

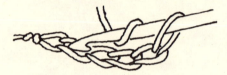

3. Wind yarn over hook and draw through a loop.
4. Yarn over hook and draw through two loops on hook (two loops now left on hook).
5. Yarn over hook and pull through remaining two loops on hook.

One double crochet made. Repeat until required number of stitches have been worked.

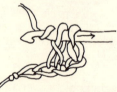

triple crochet

To triple crochet:

1. Wind yarn over hook twice.
2. Miss the first four chains from hook. Insert hook between the two loops of next chain.

3. Wind yarn over hook and draw a loop through. There should now be four loops on the hook.
4. Wind yarn over hook and pull through **two** loops on hook (now three loops on hook).
5. Repeat instruction number 4 until only one loop is left on hook.

One triple crochet made.

To finish off: *finishing*
1. Cut the yarn and draw the end through the loop left on hook.
2. Pull yarn gently to secure.

Crocheting Tips

The rules regarding wool, tension, and so on, are the same for knitting, so reread the chapter on knitted pillows before you start to crochet.

When joining in a new ball of wool, lay wool along top of row for a few inches. Crochet the next three or four stitches over the top of the new wool, then drop the old wool and continue with the new. Work in old wool the same way on the next row.

Separate strands of double knit wool or use three ply wool in the same dye to sew up your pillows. Loose backstitch or overstitch may be used.

Here is a list of the abbreviations used in the   *abbreviations*
crocheted patterns given in this book:

ch	chain	sp	space
sl st	slip stitch	rep	repeat
sc	single crochet	rnd	round
dc	double crochet	sk	skip
tr	triple crochet		

block and press   To block and press crochet, stretch work out on a padded surface to correct measurement and pin. For flat crochet, cover with a damp cloth and alternately press, then lift iron across surface. For raised patterns, hold iron just above surface to let steam through cloth.

The following patterns are simple yet attractive and make lovely pillows.

Green Hexagon Pillow

materials   8 ozs. of double knit yarn
Crochet hook to give tension below
Inner pad
  Measurement: 14" across center
  Tension: 3 dc to 1"

pattern   **Front and back alike (make two)**
Ch 8, join with sl st to form ring. Ch 1.
Rnd 1: 14 sc in ring, join to ch 1 with sl st. Ch 2.
Rnd 2: 1 dc in same sp as ch 2, 2 dc in each sc to end of rnd (30 sts). Join rnd with sl st to top of ch 2. Ch 2.
Rnd 3: * ch 1, 1 dc in each of next 5 dc, rep from * 4 times, ch 1, 1 dc in each of next 4 dc, join rnd with sl st to top of ch 2. Ch 2.
Rnd 4: * ch 2, 1 dc in each of next 2 dc, 2 dc in next dc, 1 dc in each of next 2 dc, rep from * 4 times, ch 2, 1 dc in each of next 2 dc, 2 dc in next dc, 1 dc in next dc, join rnd with a sl st to top of ch 2. Ch 2.
Rnd 5: * ch 2, 2 dc in next dc, 1 dc in each of next 4 dc, 2 dc in next dc, rep from * 4 times, ch 2, 2 dc in next dc, 1 dc in each of next 4 dc, 1 dc in next dc, join rnd with sl st to top of ch 2. Ch 2.

Rnd 6: * ch 2, 2 dc in next dc, 1 dc in each of next 6 dc, 2 dc in next dc, rep from * 4 times, ch 2, 2 dc in next dc, 1 dc in each of next 6 dc, 1 dc in next dc, join rnd with a sl st to top of ch 2. Ch 2.

Rnd 7: * ch 2, 2 dc in next dc, 1 dc in each of next 8 dc, 2 dc in next dc, rep from * 4 times, ch 2, 2 dc in next dc, 1 dc in each of next 8 dc, 1 dc in next dc, join rnd with sl st to top of ch 2. Ch 2.

Rnd 8: * ch 3, 2 dc in next dc, 1 dc in each of next 10 dc, 2 dc in next dc, rep from * 4 times, ch 3, 2 dc in next dc, 1 dc in each of next 10 dc, 1 dc in next dc, join rnd with sl st to top of ch 2. Ch 2.

Rnd 9: * ch 3, 2 dc in next dc, 1 dc in each of next 12 dc, 2 dc in next dc, rep from * 4 times, ch 3, 2 dc in next dc, 1 dc in each of next 12 dc, 1 dc in next dc, join to top of ch 2. Ch 2.

Rnd 10: * ch 3, 2 dc in next dc, 1 dc in each of next 14 dc, 2 dc in next dc, rep from * 4 times, ch 3, 2 dc in next dc, 1 dc in each of next 14 dc, 1 dc in next dc, join to top of ch 2. Ch 2.

Rnd 11: * ch 3, 2 dc in next dc, 1 dc in each of next 16 dc, 2 dc in next dc, rep from * 4 times, ch 3, 2 dc in next dc, 1 dc in each of next 16 dc, 1 dc in next dc, join to top of ch 2. Ch 2.

Rnd 12: * ch 3, 2 dc in next dc, 1 dc in each of next 18 dc, 2 dc in next dc, rep from * 4 times, ch 3, 2 dc in next dc, 1 dc in each of next 18 dc, 1 dc in next dc, join to top of ch 2.

Fasten off.

to make up

With right sides together, sew around cover leaving opening, turn right side out, insert pad, and sew up opening.

Spider Web Pillow

materials

8 ozs. of craft wool
Crochet hook to give tension below
Inner pad
  Measurements: 15" diameter (stretched)
  Tension: 3 dc to 1"

pattern   **Front and back alike (make two)**
Ch 8, join with a sl st to form ring.

Rnd 1:   15 sc in ring, join rnd with a sl st. Ch 2.

Rnd 2:   * ch 1, 1 dc in next sc, rep from * to end of rnd, join with a sl st to top of ch 2. (16 dc) Ch 2.

Rnd 3:   * ch 2, 1 dc in next dc, rep from * 15 times, ch 2, join to top of ch 2 with a sl st. Ch 2.

Rnd 4:   * ch 3, 1 dc next dc, rep from * 15 times, ch 3, join to top of ch 2. Ch 2.

Rnd 5:   * ch 4, 1 dc in next dc, rep from * 15 times, ch 4, join to top of ch 2. Ch 2.

Rnd 6:   * ch 5, 1 dc in next dc, rep from * 15 times, ch 5, join to top of ch 2. Ch 2.

Rnd 7:   * ch 6, 1 dc in next dc, rep from * 15 times, ch 6, join to top of ch 2. Ch 2.

Rnd 8:   * ch 7, 1 dc in next dc, rep from * 15 times, ch 7, join to top of ch 2. Ch 2.

Rnd 9:   * ch 8, 1 dc in next dc, rep from * 15 times, ch 8, join to top of ch 2. Ch 2.

Rnd 10:   * ch 9, 1 dc in next dc, rep from * 15 times, ch 9, join to top of ch 2.

Fasten off.

boxing strip   To crochet the boxing strip, ch 6. 1 dc in 2nd ch from hook, 1 dc in each ch to end of row. Ch 2. * Work 1 dc in each dc to end of row, ch 2, turn. Rep from * till strip will fit around cover piece. Fasten off.

to make up   Join short edges of boxing strip. Sew one side of boxing around one cover piece. Sew other side of boxing to other side of cover piece leaving opening. Insert pad and sew up opening.

Bolster

materials   4 ozs. of craft yarn in orange
4 ozs. of craft yarn in green
Crochet hook to give tension below
Inner pad
   Measurements: 15" long, 6" in diameter
   Tension: 3 dc to 1"

Body

With green wool ch 45.

Row 1:   1 dc in 2nd ch from hook, 1 dc in each ch to end of row. Ch 2, turn.

Row 2:   1 dc in each dc across row, ch 2, turn.

Rep row 2, 7 times, then work 9 rows of dc in orange wool and another 9 in green wool.

Fasten off.

End pieces (make two)

With orange wool ch 6, join with sl st to form ring. Ch 1.

Rnd 1:   9 sc in ring, join rnd with sl st to top of ch 1. Ch 2.

Rnd 2:   2 dc in each of next 8 sc, 1 dc in next sc, join with sl st to top of ch 2. Ch 2.

Rnd 3:   1 dc in same sp as ch 2, * 1 dc in next dc, 2 dc in next dc, rep from * to last dc, 1 dc in last dc, join with sl st to top of ch 2. Ch 2.

Rnd 4:   * ch 1, 1 dc in next dc, rep from * 25 times, ch 1, join with sl st to top of ch 2. Ch 2.

Rnd 5:   * ch 1, 2 dc in next dc, rep from * to last dc, ch 1, 2 dc in next dc, ch 1, join to top of ch 2 with a sl st.

Fasten off.

Fold body piece in half crosswise, and sew a few inches at both ends, on long edge. Sew one circle to each end of bolster and turn so that seams are on the inside. Insert pad and sew up opening.

Mauve and Purple Square

4 ozs. of craft yarn in mauve
4 ozs. of craft yarn in purple
Crochet hook to give tension below
Inner pad
   Measurements: 12" x 10"
   Tension: 3 dc to 1"

pattern   Ch 60.
Row 1:   1 dc in 2nd ch from hook, 1 dc in each ch to end of row. Ch 2, turn.
Row 2:   1 dc in each dc to end of row, ch 2, turn.
Rep row 2 till work measures 6". Work another 6" in purple wool.
Fasten off.

to make up   Fold piece in half, crosswise, with right sides together. Sew along two sides, turn right side out, insert pad, and sew up opening.

Red Triangle

materials   4 ozs. of double knit yarn
Crochet hook to give tension below
Inner pad
   Measurements: 18" square
   Tension: 4 dc to 1"

pattern   Ch 6, join with a sl st to form ring. Ch 3.
Rnd 1:   2 tr, into ring, ch 4, * 3 tr in ring, ch 4, rep from * twice, join to top of ch 3 with a sl st. Ch 3.
Rnd 2:   * ch 3, (3 tr, ch 4, 3 tr, in ch 4 sp) * rep from * to * twice, ch 3, 3 tr, ch 4, 2 tr in ch 4 sp, join to top of ch 3 with a sl st. Ch 3.
Keep on working in rounds making ch 3 across each 3 tr, 3 tr in each ch 3 sp, and 3 tr, ch 4, 3 tr, in each ch 4 sp (corner). Join rnds with a sl st and work ch 3 before beginning new rnd. Contine until work measures 18" square.
Fasten off.

to make up   Fold square in half to form a triangle. Work one row of sc around one side, insert pad and crochet along other side. Make three tassels as described on page 32 and sew one to each corner of pillow.

Blue
Striped
Fringed
Pillow

materials

4 ozs. of double knit yarn in light blue
4 ozs. of double knit yarn in medium blue
8 ozs. of double knit yarn in dark blue
Crochet hook to give tension below
Inner pad
    Measurements: 15" x 12"
    Tension: 4 dc to 1"

Front and back alike (make two)

pattern

With light wool ch 48.
Row 1:   1 dc in 2nd ch from hook, 1 dc in each ch
    to end of row. Ch 2, turn.
Row 2:   1 dc in each dc to end of row. Ch 2, turn.
Rep row 2 till work measures 1¼". Now work 1¼"
    stripes as follows: medium, dark, light, medium,
    dark, dark, medium, light, dark, medium, light.
Work should measure 15".
Fasten off.

    With right sides together, sew along three sides.

to make up

Turn right side out, insert pad, then sew up other
side.
    Make fringe as described for Gold Moss Stitch
(knitted) Pillow. Use dark blue wool for fringe.

White
Pillow

materials

6 ozs. of double knit yarn
Crochet hook to give tension below
Inner pad
    Measurements: 15" x 12"
    Tension: 4 dc to 1"

pattern **Front and back alike (make two)**
Ch 60.

Row 1: 1 dc in 2nd ch from hook, 1 dc in each ch to end of row. (60 dc) Ch 2. Turn.

Row 2: 1 dc in each dc across row. Ch 2, turn.

Rows 3–8: Same as row 2.

Row 9: 1 dc in each of next 29 dc, ch 4, sk next 4 dc, 1 dc in each dc to end of row. Ch 2, turn.

Row 10: 1 dc in each of next 21 dc, ch 4, sk next 4 dc, 4 dc in ch 4 sp, 1 dc in each dc to end of row. Ch 2, turn.

Row 11: 1 dc in each of next 21 dc, ch 4, sk next 4 dc, 1 dc in next 8 dc, 4 dc in ch 4 sp, ch 4, sk next 4 dc, 1 dc in each dc to end of row. Ch 2, turn.

Row 12: 1 dc in each of next 13 dc, ch 4, sk next 4 dc, 4 dc in ch 4 sp, 1 dc in each of next 8 dc, ch 4, sk next 4 dc, 4 dc in ch 4 sp, 1 dc in each dc to end of row. Ch 2, turn.

Row 13: 1 dc in each of next 13 dc, ch 4, sk next 4 dc, 1 dc in each of next 8 dc, 4 dc in ch 4 sp, ch 4, sk next 4 dc, 1 dc in each of next 8 dc, 4 dc in ch 4 sp, ch 4, sk next 4 dc, 1 dc in each dc to end of row. Ch 2, turn.

Row 14: 1 dc in each of next 5 dc, ch 4, sk next 4 dc, 4 dc in ch 4 sp, 1 dc in each of next 8 dc, ch 4, sk next 4 dc, 4 dc in ch 4 sp, 1 dc in each of next 8 dc, ch 4, sk next 4 dc, 4 dc in ch 4 sp, 1 dc in each dc to end of row. Ch 2, turn.

Row 15: 1 dc in each of next 5 dc, ch 4, sk next 4 dc, 1 dc in each of next 8 dc, 4 dc in ch 4 sp, ch 4, sk next 4 dc, 1 dc in each of next 8 dc, 4 dc in ch 4 sp, ch 4, sk next 4 dc, 1 dc in each of next 8 dc, 4 dc in ch 4 sp, 1 dc in each dc to end of row. Ch 2, turn.

Row 16: 1 dc in each of next 13 dc, ch 4, sk next 4 dc, 4 dc in ch 4 sp, 1 dc in each of next 8 dc, ch 4, sk next 4 dc, 4 dc in ch 4 sp, 1 dc in each of next 8 dc, ch 4, sk next 4 dc, 4 dc in ch 4 sp, 1 dc in each dc to end of row. Ch 2, turn.

Row 17: 1 dc in each of next 9 dc, 4 dc in ch 4 sp, ch 4, sk next 4 dc, 1 dc in each of next 8 dc, 4 dc in ch 4 sp, ch 4, sk next 4 dc, 1 dc in each dc to end of row. Ch 2, turn.

Row 18: 1 dc in each of next 21 dc, ch 4, sk next 4 dc, 4 dc in ch 4 sp, 1 dc in each of next 8 dc, ch 4, sk next 4 dc, 4 dc in ch 4 sp, 1 dc in each dc to end of row. Ch 2, turn.

Row 19: 1 dc in each of next 17 dc, 4 dc in ch 4 sp, ch 4, sk next 4 dc, 1 dc in each of next 8 dc, 4 dc in ch 4 sp, 1 dc in each dc to end of row. Ch 2, turn.

Row 20: 1 dc in each of next 29 dc, ch 4, sk next 4 dc, 4 dc in ch 4 sp, 1 dc in each dc to end of row. Ch 2, turn.

Row 21: 1 dc in each of next 25 dc, 4 dc in ch 4 sp, 1 dc in each dc to end of row. Ch 2, turn.

Rows 22–28: As row 2.

Fasten off.

to make up

With right sides together, sew along three edges, turn right side out, insert pad, and sew up opening.

Use a brightly colored or black inner pad to show up pattern on pillow.

Patchwork Pillow

materials

8 ozs. of double knit yarn in 8 different colors
4 ozs. of double knit yarn in black for fringe
Crochet hook to give tension below
Inner pad
  Measurements: 12″ square
  Tension: 4 dc to 1″

pattern

Make 16 squares 3″ x 3″ for each side of cover
Ch 12.

Row 1: 1 dc in 2nd ch from hook, 1 dc in each ch across row. Ch 2, turn.

Row 2: 1 dc in each dc to end of row. Ch 2, turn.

Rep row 2 until work measures 3″.

Fasten off.

to make up

Arrange squares in different patterns till you get the combination you like best. Sew squares together. With right sides of cover together sew around three edges, turn right side out, and insert pad. Sew up opening. Make fringe as for Gold Moss Stitch (knitted) Pillow.

flower fantasies

Crocheted flowers and flowers made on a small loom are used on these pretty pillows.

Plastic looms with adjustable pegs are available at hobby and wool shops for only a few dollars. One loom will make flowers of several sizes. Flowers are made by winding and crisscrossing yarn around the pegs. The center of the flower is worked with a needle and contrasting yarn. The pegs are then removed and the flower is finished off and ready to use. The thickness of the flower depends on how many times the yarn is wound around the pegs.

Flowers may be scattered on pillow or arranged, and can be sewn on before or after pillow is made up.

Just about any fabric can be used for the pillows. Solid colored fabric is better than patterned, although I have put flowers on check fabric for a very pretty pillow.

Pillows may be ruffled, piped, flanged, or boxed. Here are six pillows you might try.

Daisy Pillow
materials

2 pieces of fabric 13″ x 15″
White and yellow double knit wool
Inner pad
   Following instructions on package, make seven 2″ white flowers with yellow centers on loom. Make up pillow cover as for regular pillow, then sew one flower in center of front cover. Sew other flowers around this one making a small cluster.

Poppy Pillow
materials

2 pieces of linen 13″ x 17″
Red and green double knit wool
Inner pad
   Follow instructions on package and make three 3½″ red flowers with red centers on loom. Place on pillow cover as shown in cover photo. Sew in place. Stem stitch stalks in green wool and satin stitch leaves in green. Make up cover as for regular pillow.

Bolster Pillow
materials

1 piece of fabric 19″ x 13″
2 circular pieces with 6½″ diameters
Double knit wool in assorted colors
Inner pad
   Follow directions on package and make 14 2″ flowers in assorted colors. Make up regular bolster using ½″ seams. Sew seven flowers on each end; one in the middle and six around it.

Half Moon Pillow
materials

2 pieces of fabric, half moon shaped. (Fold circle with 22″ diameter in half and cut along fold.)
Double knit wool in assorted colors

Inner pad

Follow directions on package and make enough 2″ and 2½″ flowers in assorted colors to cover all of pillow. Make up pillow and sew on flowers. Pillow will take about 20 flowers of each size.

Gingham Pillow

materials   2 pieces green checked gingham 13″ x 13″
1½ yds. dark green piping
#4.50 (international size) crochet hook
White and yellow double knit wool
Inner pad

Make up a regular piped pillow. Crochet 24 petals and 3 centers. Make each flower out of eight petals and one center. Sew onto cover separately.

pattern   **Petal**

With white wool ch 9.

1 sc in 2nd ch from hook, 1 sc in each of next 2 ch, 1 dc in each of next 2 ch, 1 tr in each of next 2 ch, 5 tr in next ch (corner).

Working along bottom of previous sts cont as follows: 1 tr in each of next 2 ch, 1 dc in each of next 2 ch, 1 sc in next 3 ch, 1 sc same sp as first sc.

Fasten off.

Center

With yellow wool ch 4, join with slip stitch to form ring. Ch 2. 9 dc in ring, join to top of ch 2 with a sl st.

Fasten off.

Circular Pillow

materials   2 circular pieces of fabric with 13″ diameters
Double knit wool in contrasting color
Inner pad

Make 25 2″ flowers following directions on package of loom. Make up a regular circular pillow, using ½" seams. Sew 18 flowers side by side around outer edge of pillow, and 7 in a cluster in center.

mod pillows

30

The thing that sets mod pillows apart from other pillows is actually the fabric. It is the design that is mod. Big, oversized, splashy prints, stripes, geometrics, abstracts, stylized, and occasionally psychedelic or free-form patterns come under this heading. So do loosely woven fabrics and fabrics with interesting or unusual textures such as fur, leather, vinyl, and synthetics.

Colors are usually stark and bold—black, white, scarlet, electric blue, shocking pink, and bright yellow. But sometimes earthy or neutral tones are seen.

Modern furniture has smooth, sleek lines. Mod pillows—squares, rectangles and triangles—go well in these rooms. Giant floor pillows are popular too. Some pillows are understuffed to give a floppy effect.

Although most pillows have plain knife edges, some are decorated with an extra long shaggy fringe.

Following are six design suggestions for mod pillows.

Two-toned Pillow

2 pieces of black fabric each 9" x 9"   *materials*
2 pieces of white fabric each 9" x 9"
Inner pad

Sew one black square to one white one with a 1" seam. Repeat with the other two squares. Now make up as for regular pillow.

Fur Patchwork Pillow

9 - 5" x 5" dark fur squares   *materials*
9 - 5" x 5" light fur squares
Inner pad

Sew nine squares together with ½" seams as shown. Repeat with the other nine squares, then make up as for regular pillow.

Fringed Triangle

materials 2 triangular pieces of wool fabric 17″ x 17″ x 17″
1½ yds. of extra long shag fringe
Inner pad

Make up as for regular fringed pillow using 1″ seams.

Floppy Pillow

materials 2 pieces of fabric 15″ x 15″
Stuffing

Sew cover with right sides together around three sides (½″ seam). Stuff to produce a floppy pillow. Sew up opening. If you prefer you can make an inner pad the same way with unbleached cotton.

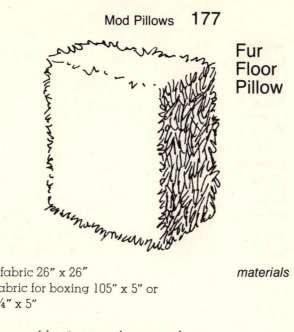

Fur
Floor
Pillow

2 pieces of fur fabric 26″ x 26″   *materials*
1 piece of fur fabric for boxing 105″ x 5″ or
    4 pieces 26¼″ x 5″
Inner pad
    Sew four pieces of boxing together to make one
long strip. Make up a regular boxed pillow.

Geometric
Pillow

2 pieces of fabric with geometric design   *materials*
    each 13″ x 17″
Inner pad
    Make up as for regular pillow.

bolsters

31

Bolsters are also very popular now. They make a welcome change from the ordinary flat pillow and are surprisingly simple to construct. When I tackled my first bolster, the pieces went together so easily and quickly that I thought there was something wrong with the pillow and kept on looking at it to see if I had forgotten anything.

A bolster takes its shape from the end pieces, which may be circular, triangular, or square. The sausage bolster has no ends as such, it is just sausage shaped. The body of the bolster can be any length from 8″ and up. The diameter is usually about 6″ to 8″.

Any fabric can be made into a bolster and the pillows may be decorated in a number of different ways. Frills, piping, fringe, tassels, or buttons are fine for the ends; and braiding, appliqué, embroidery, smocking, can decorate the body.

Plain and print fabric can be combined, as for example: patterned body with plain ends; patterned body and ends with a plain frill; or panels of plain and print fabric with plain ends.

You could make your own inner pad or buy one ready made. The ready-made ones, however, are quite expensive so it would be wiser to make your own.

Here, are 12 bolster designs decorated as follows: each made from three-quarters of a yard of fabric.

An 8" patterned section in a solid body piece with button ends.

bolster designs

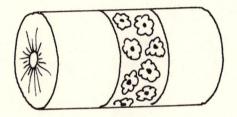

Plaid body with plain ends and contrasting piping.

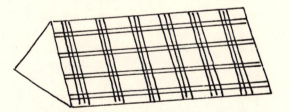

Patchwork body with plain ends.

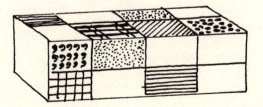

Lengths of braid with lines of rick-rack on each side.
All are sewn into position before cover is completed.

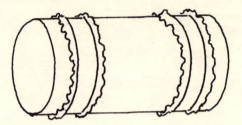

Plain triangular bolster with a tassel at each end.

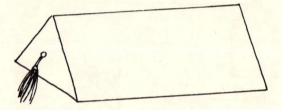

Rick-rack, piping, and buttons adorn this one.

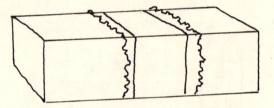

A 1" wide plain ruffle (see page 31) around each
end of a patterned body.

A 1″ wide braid sewn onto all three sides of tri-angle.

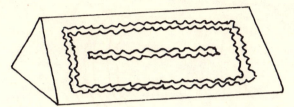

Pom-pom fringe around ends.

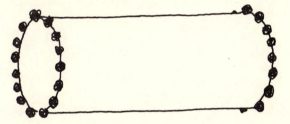

Two strands of extra thick yarn slip stitched around ends and tied into bows at top and bottom.

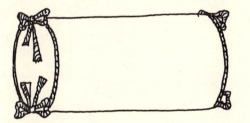

Four pieces of 6″ x 19″ fabric sewn together down long sides with piping inserted in ½″ seams—ends are piped, also.

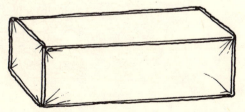

Plain fur bolster.

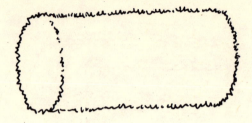

Shams, pallet or squab cushions, stool pillows, and bath pillows are grouped under the heading of miscellaneous pillows.

Many people have kitchen chairs and stools that they would like pillows for, and frilly shams look lovely on a bed.

Informal fabrics can be used and pillows can be ruffled, piped, fringed, appliquéd, embroidered, and so on.

I have included directions for making a sham, stool pillow, bath pillow, and kitchen chair pillow.

Terrycloth is ideal for the bath pillow but it could be made from any other absorbent fabric.

Kitchen Chair Pillow

You will need two pieces of fabric in the shape of your chair seat, plus 1" all around.

to ruffle   If you want a ruffle, measure around two sides and the front of cover piece. Total up the inches and then double them and add 2". This will give you the length of ruffle fabric, the width will depend on how wide you want the ruffle. Average width would be 2½". So you would need 5" plus another 2" for seam allowance giving you a total of 7" for width of ruffle. Make as for regular ruffle and sew around front and sides of pillow only.

tie tapes   To add tie tapes, fold a piece of tape 16" long in half and sew folded edge to back edge of bottom cover piece, on right sides of fabric, a few inches from each end (1" seam) as shown. Make up pillow as for regular one.

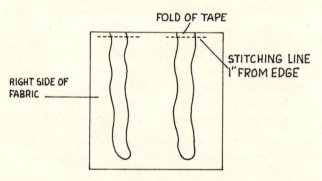

piping   Piping should go all around pillow. Measure around edges of cover piece and add a few extra inches. Divide by 36 to give you the number of yards of piping that you'll need.

Stool Pillow

Stool pillows are regular, round, ruffled pillows with tapes added to tie them onto a stool.

Sew four single pieces of tape at equal distance from each other on bottom cover piece, on right side of fabric. Short edge of tape should be even with cover edge as shown. Tapes should be long enough to tie under stool. Make up as for regular ruffled pillow.

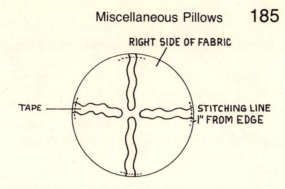

RIGHT SIDE OF FABRIC

TAPE

STITCHING LINE
1" FROM EDGE

Sham

Shams are frilled covers for bed size pillows.
  Average size: 15" x 24"

Front cover piece: 17" x 26"   *materials*
Back: cut one piece 12½" x 26" (top half)
      cut one piece 15½" x 26" (bottom)
  Press under 1" on bottom of top piece, and 1" on
top of bottom piece. Stitch. Press under another 3"
on both and stitch up sides as shown in fig. 1.

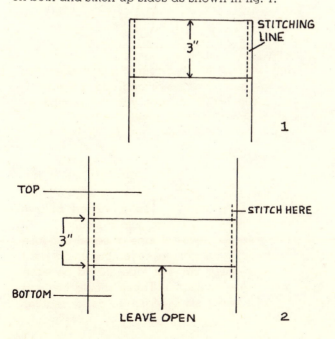

STITCHING
LINE

3"

1

TOP

3"

STITCH HERE

BOTTOM

LEAVE OPEN   2

Overlap top pieces over bottom piece for 3". Pin and stitch along sides as shown in fig. 2. Now use as regular cover piece. Pillow slips inside "envelope" opening.

For ruffle you will need a fabric of 158" x 8". Sew shorter lengths together to obtain long piece. Make up as for regular ruffle.

Bath Pillow

materials 1 piece of fabric (terrycloth) 14" x 18"
2 circular pieces 5" in diameter
Inner pad

Make up as for regular bolster using 1" seams.

This is a nice little bolster, ideal for relaxing in the tub or for comfort when you have a head full of rollers.